Mathematics Practice Tests

Level 6
Mathematics

Michael W Priestley

First edition 2013
Reprinted 2013 (twice)

ISBN 978-981-07-3237-0

Welcome to studySMART!

■SCHOLASTIC

Mathematics Practice Tests is designed to help your child prepare to take mid-year and end-of-year tests.

Each practice test has 15 multiple-choice problems, 20 short response problems and 9–11 extended response problems. Your child should take 80–90 minutes to complete each practice test.

The questions in each test assess
- *Knowledge:* the ability to recall mathematical facts, concepts, rules and formulae, and to perform straightforward computations

- *Comprehension:* the ability to interpret data and use mathematical concepts, rules or formulae and to solve routine mathematical problems

- *Application and Analytical Skills:* the ability to analyze data and/or apply mathematical concepts, rules or formulae in complex situations

At the back of this book you will find a **Skills and Strategies Index** and an **Answer Key**.

The Skills and Strategies Index
- categorizes the problems according to Knowledge, Comprehension, and Application and Analytical Skills categories,
- lists the mathematical concepts and skills measured and the test problems that measure each skill, and
- lists suggested problem-solving strategies for some extended response problems.

This index may be helpful to you in determining what kinds of problems your child answered incorrectly, what skills he may be having trouble with, and which areas he may need further instruction in.

To score a test, please refer to the corresponding Answer Key, which lists the correct response to each problem and provides worked solutions to extended response problems.

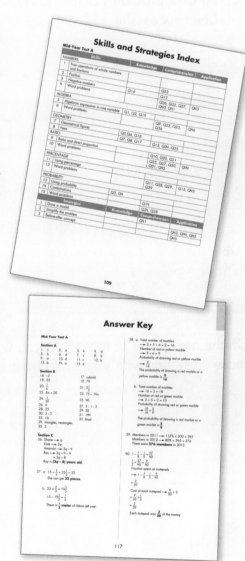

How to use this book

1. Ensure your child has the necessary tools such as a ruler, protractor, set-square etc.

2. Tell your child how much time he has to complete the practice test. Encourage him to work quickly and carefully, and to keep track of the remaining time — just as he would in a real testing session.

3. Do not allow your child to use a calculator.

4. To score a practice test, go through the test and mark each problem answered correctly. Add the number of correct answers to find your child's test score. Record the score on the contents page to keep track of your child's progress.
    You might want to have your child correct his own tests. This will give him a chance to see where he made mistakes and what he needs to do to improve his scores on the next test. Provide remediation as necessary.

5. Parallel problems across tests allow you to assess if remediation has been successful.

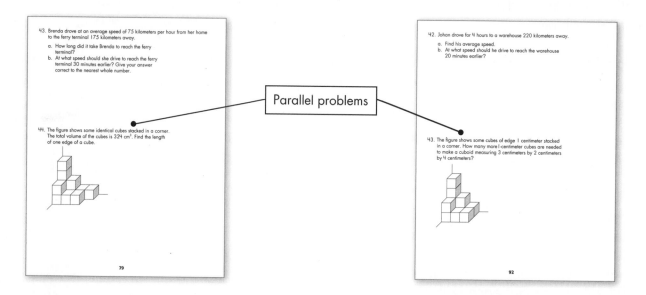

On the next page of this book, you will find test-taking tips. You may want to share these tips with your child before he begins working on the practice tests.

A Note to Parents

Dear Parents

Children are more likely to be successful learners of mathematics when parents actively support their learning. By playing an active role in your child's learning, you will reinforce his skills and nurture a positive attitude towards mathematics.

Take some time to go through these test-taking strategies with your child so that he becomes familiar with them. Help your child apply these strategies when taking mathematics tests.

- **Learn the vocabulary**
  Become familiar with all mathematical terms that may appear in the test (for example *area*, *remainder*, *speed*, etc.) so that you understand what you are being asked to do.

- **Underline key words**
  Underline the key words after reading the problem carefully. Are you asked to find the sum? The angle measure?

- **Choosing the right option in a multiple-choice problem**
  Read the problem carefully then read all the answer options. Eliminate the options that you know are incorrect. If you are still unsure of the final answer, substitute the unknown in the problem with the remaining options and check if the answer is correct.

- **Identify the unnecessary information**
  Word problems sometimes give you more information than you need to solve the problem. Seek what you need and ignore the unnecessary information.

- **Use problem-solving strategies**
  Often there is more than one way to solve a problem. Apply a strategy that works best for a problem, e.g. drawing a picture, making a list, etc.

- **Use your time wisely**
  Plan how much time you should spend on each problem. This helps ensure that you have ample time to complete the test and do a thorough check of your work.

- **Check your work**
  When you have completed the test, go over as many problems as you can, making sure your answers are correct. Never rush through a mathematics test.

Contents

Mid-Year Test A

Section A

Questions 1 to 15 carry 1 point each. For each question, choose the correct answer and write its letter in the parentheses provided.

1. Simplify $5d + 11 - 2d$.
   a. $7d + 11$
   b. $7d - 11$
   c. $3d + 11$
   d. $3d - 11$ (   )

2. If $x = 4$, what is the value of $10 + 3x$?
   a. 22   b. 20
   c. 17   d. 13   (   )

Use the table below to answer questions 3 and 4.

Kendra built a race track for marbles. She pours some marbles through a funnel onto the track.

Color	Number of Marbles
Green	5
Blue	7
Red	2
Purple	6

3. Which colored marble is most likely to finish first?
   a. green   b. blue
   c. red   d. purple   (   )

4. What is the probability of a red marble finishing first?
   a. $\dfrac{1}{4}$ b. $\dfrac{1}{5}$
   c. $\dfrac{1}{8}$ d. $\dfrac{1}{10}$ (   )

5. PQRS is a square. What is the measure of $\angle PRQ$?

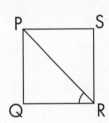

   a. 30°   b. 45°
   c. 90°   d. 180°   (   )

6. The trapezoid below is not drawn to scale. Find the measure of ∠p.

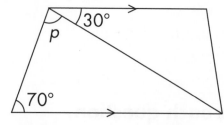

a. 30°   b. 60°
c. 70°   d. 80°   ( )

7. Which solid is formed by this net?

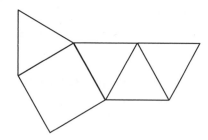

a. cube   b. prism
c. pyramid   d. cuboid   ( )

8. Which solid below has six faces?

a.   b.

c.   d.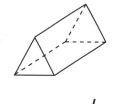

( )

9. A cardboard box can hold 6 mugs. How many boxes are needed to hold 24c mugs?
a. 4c   b. 18c
c. 20c   d. 30c   ( )

10. A box of erasers was shared among Karen, Lisa, and Maria in the ratio 2 : 5 : 6. What fraction of the box of erasers did Maria receive?

a. $\frac{2}{5}$ b. $\frac{6}{7}$

c. $\frac{5}{13}$ d. $\frac{6}{13}$ ( )

11. Anusha has finished baking 42 oatmeal muffins for a bake sale. If this is 35% of the total order, how many oatmeal muffins does she have to bake in all?
a. 162 oatmeal muffins
b. 142 oatmeal muffins
c. 120 oatmeal muffins
d. 83 oatmeal muffins   ( )

12. Which number line shows the sum of −2 and 4?

a.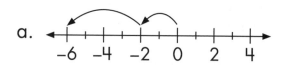

b.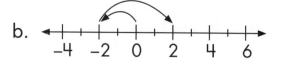

c.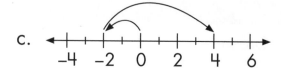

d.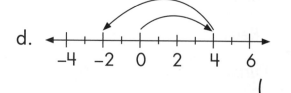

( )

13. A restaurant menu offers 4 kinds of sandwiches, 3 kinds of salads, and 2 kinds of drinks.

Menu		
Sandwiches 4	Salads 3	Drinks 2

How many different combinations of 1 sandwich, 1 salad, and 1 drink can be made?

a. 24   b. 20
c. 12   d. 9   (   )

14. Which type of solid has five faces?
a. sphere
b. square pyramid
c. cube
d. cone   (   )

15. A group of students raised money for a class trip. 24% of the money was earned by washing cars. What information do you need to find the amount raised by washing cars?
a. the cost per car for the wash
b. the number of cars washed
c. the number of students
d. the total amount of money raised   (   )

Section B

For questions 16 to 35, each answer carries 1 point.
Write your answer in the answer blank provided.

16. What number does *x* represent?

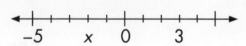

Ans: _____

17. What is the solid formed by this net?

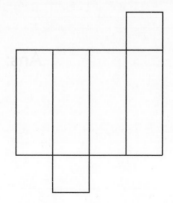

Ans: _____

9

18. The rhombus below is not drawn to scale.
    Find the measure of ∠u.

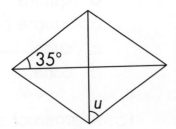

Ans: _____°

19. Find the value of 9w + 15 – w, when w = 8.

Ans: _____

20. The ratio of the number of ducks to the number of
    swans in a pond is 6 : 1. What fraction of the ducks
    are the swans?

Ans: _____

21. The ratio of the mass of flour to the mass of meat
    used in baking a pie is 2 : 5. How many times
    as much meat as flour is used?

Ans: _____

22. Derek ran x meters. Jules ran 6 times the distance
    Derek ran. Andrew ran 20 more meters than Jules.
    How far did Andrew run?

Ans: _____ m

23. Diya had 75 postcards. She gave 2*n* postcards to each of her 7 friends. How many postcards does she have left? Give your answer in terms of *n*.

Ans: _____ postcards

24. A store gave out 300 tickets for a lucky draw to win a prize. Ryan got 6 tickets. What is the probability that he will win the prize?

Ans: _____

25. Hisham has $\frac{1}{4}$ as many stamps as stickers. If he has 10 stamps, how many stickers does he have?

Ans: _____ stickers

26. A group of people shared $\frac{9}{15}$ kilogram of tomatoes.

Each person received $\frac{1}{10}$ kilogram of tomatoes.

How many people were there in the group?

Ans: _____ people

27. There are 5 times as many counters in Bag A as in Bag B. Bag C has half the total number of counters in Bag A and Bag B. What is the ratio of the number of counters in Bag A to Bag B to Bag C?

Ans: _____

28. Liana worked for a total of 48 hours in March. In April, she worked for a total of 60 hours. What was the percentage increase in the hours she worked?

Ans: _____%

29. In a race, John had to run a certain number of rounds around a track. After running 4 rounds, he had 80% of the race left to complete. How many rounds around the track was the entire race?

Ans: _____ rounds

30. Sylvia had $\frac{3}{4}$ kilogram of cherries while Rita had $\frac{1}{2}$ kilogram of cherries. Express the amount of cherries that Sylvia had as a ratio of the amount of cherries Rita had.

Ans: _____

31. Jessie gave all of her card collection to her two friends in the ratio 7 : 1. If Jessie had 192 cards, what is the difference in the number of cards her friends received?

Ans: _____ cards

32. There were 10 liters of rainwater in a tank. Peter used $\frac{2}{5}$ of it and filled several pots equally with the remainder. Each pot has $\frac{3}{8}$ liter of rainwater. How many pots did he fill?

Ans: _____ pots

33. Five people are standing in a line at the video store. Pete is at the front of the line. Stan is directly in front of Brad. Alison is between Stan and Erin. Who is last in line?

Ans: _____

34. What two shapes are the faces of the solid below?

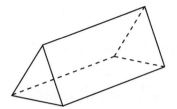

Ans: _____

35. How many rectangular faces does the solid below have?

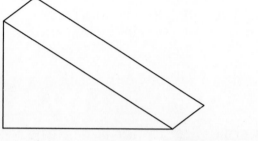

Ans: _____ rectangular faces

Section C

For questions 36 to 46, each answer carries 1 point.
Write your answer in the space provided.
Show your work.

36. Shane is q years old. Kate is 3 times as old as Shane.
    Amanda is 4 years younger than Kate. Ray is 4 years
    younger than Amanda. In terms of q, how old is Ray?

37. Maya has a roll of ribbon 15 meters long. She needs to cut the entire roll into smaller pieces measuring $\frac{2}{3}$ meter.

   a. What is the greatest number of the smaller pieces she can get?
   b. What is the length of ribbon that will be left over?

38. A bag contains 3 red marbles, 5 green marbles, 6 yellow marbles, and 2 black marbles. Gina draws a marble at random from the bag.

   a. What is the probability that she will draw a red marble or a yellow marble?
   b. If she adds 2 more red marbles, what is the probability of drawing a red or green marble?

39. A swimming club had 300 members in 2010. In 2011, the membership increased by 15%. In 2012, the membership dropped by 20% from the previous year. How many members were there in 2012?

40. I spent $\frac{1}{8}$ of my money on a dress, $\frac{1}{5}$ on a book, and $\frac{1}{3}$ of the remainder on a toy. Then I bought 3 similar notepads with the rest of the money. What fraction of the money was the cost of each notepad?

41. $\frac{1}{5}$ of Tom's height is equal to $\frac{1}{3}$ of Jerry's height.
If their total height is 320 centimeters, what is Jerry's height?

42. Carrie has $\frac{3}{5}$ as many stuffed animals as dolls.

    a. What is the ratio of the number of stuffed animals to the number of dolls to the total number of toys?

    b. If there are 36 stuffed animals, how many toys are there in all?

43. A lemon pie and a cherry pie have a total mass of
900 grams. Jackie bought 6 lemon pies and 4 cherry
pies, with a total mass of 4800 grams.
What is the mass of 2 lemon pies?
Express your answer in kilograms and grams.

44. The ratio of the number of parrots to the number of canaries
in a pet shop is 3 : 4. The ratio of the number of finches
to the number of canaries is 1 : 6. If there are 66 parrots
and finches altogether, how many canaries are there?

45. 64% of the students in a school hall were girls. When 25% of the boys left the hall, there were 810 boys remaining in the hall. How many students were in the hall at first?

46. The perimeter of Square S is 3 times the perimeter of Rectangle T. The length of Rectangle T is 3 times its breadth.

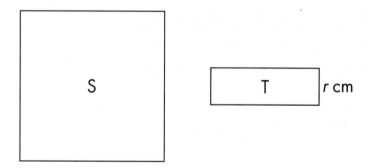

a. Express the perimeter of Square S in terms of r.
b. If $r = 5$, what is the area of Square S?

Date: _____

Mid-Year Test B

Section A

Questions 1 to 15 carry 1 point each. For each question, choose the correct answer and write its letter in the parentheses provided.

1. Simplify $3x + 5x - 7$.
   a. $3x + 2$
   b. $3x - 2$
   c. $8x - 7$
   d. $8x + 12$ ( )

2. Find the value of $5 \times 4y$ when $y = 2$.
   a. 9   b. 10
   c. 20   d. 40 ( )

3. What number is the arrow pointing at?

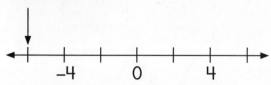

   a. -4 b. -5
   c. -6 d. -8 ( )

4. Lara placed some letter tiles in a box.

Letter	Number of Tiles
E	12
T	6
A	4
R	8

If she draws a tile without looking, what is the probability that she will get a 'T'?
   a. $\dfrac{1}{4}$ b. $\dfrac{1}{5}$
   c. $\dfrac{4}{5}$ d. $\dfrac{1}{30}$ ( )

19

5. The trapezoid below is not drawn to scale. Find the measure of ∠BCD.

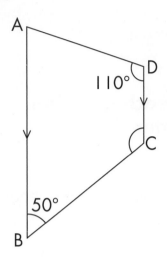

a. 130°   b. 120°
c. 100°   d. 70°   (   )

6. Which solid below has 4 faces?

a.
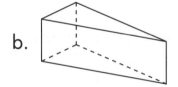

b.
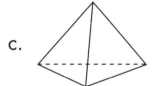

c.
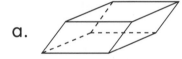

d.
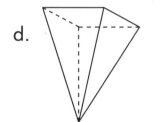

(   )

7. Which of the solids below has more than five faces?
   a. cylinder
   b. square pyramid
   c. triangular pyramid
   d. cuboid   (   )

8. Which figure below shows the net of a cuboid?

a.
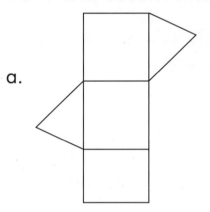

b.
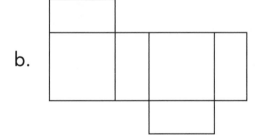

c.
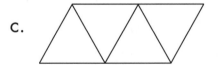

d.
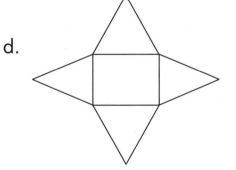

(   )

9. The figure below is not drawn to scale. DEF is an isosceles triangle and EFG is a straight line. What is the measure of ∠q?

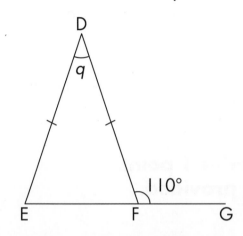

a. 30°   b. 40°
c. 50°   d. 60°   ( )

10. Shah cuts 2 pizzas into equal-sized pieces. Each piece was $\frac{1}{8}$ of a pizza. How many pieces did he cut the pizzas into?
a. 16   b. 10
c. 8   d. 4   ( )

11. The mass of a grapefruit is $\frac{4}{7}$ of the mass of a melon. What is the ratio of the mass of the grapefruit to the total mass of the two fruits?
a. 4 : 11   b. 4 : 7
c. 11 : 4   d. 7 : 4 ( )

12. A florist sold 140 roses on Sunday. He sold 40% more roses on Monday. How many more roses did he sell on Monday than on Sunday?
a. 40   b. 56
c. 180   d. 196   ( )

13. Which number sentence below matches this number line?

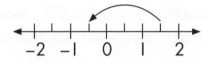

a. 2 – 0.5 = 1.5
b. –0.5 + 2 = 1.5
c. 1.5 – 2 = –0.5
d. 2 – 1.5 = 0.5   ( )

14. Selma made 2 kinds of beverages, 4 kinds of sandwiches, and 3 kinds of cookies for a fundraiser.

Beverages	Sandwiches	Cookies
2	4	3

How many different combinations of a beverage, a sandwich, and a cookie can be made?
a. 9   b. 14
c. 18   d. 24   ( )

15. Franny rolls two number cubes numbered 1 to 6. What is the probability that she will roll a sum of 12 on one try?

a. $\dfrac{1}{18}$ b. $\dfrac{1}{30}$

c. $\dfrac{1}{36}$ d. $\dfrac{12}{35}$ ( )

Section B

For questions 16 to 35, each answer carries 1 point. Write your answer in the answer blank provided.

16. What number does x represent?

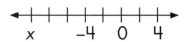

Ans: _____

17. Name the solid formed by this net.

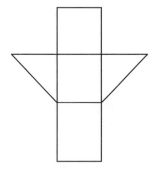

Ans: _____

18. The figure below is not drawn to scale. PQRU is a parallelogram. PUT and QRS are straight lines. What is the measure of $\angle PQR$?

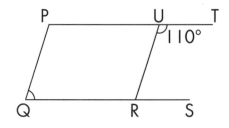

Ans:_____°

22

19. If $e = 2$, find the value of $5e - 3 + 2e + 5$.

Ans: _____

20. Budi randomly picks a ball from a bag containing 3 green balls, 2 red balls, and 5 black balls. Which colored ball will he most likely pick?

Ans: _____ ball

21. The ratio of the number of sunflowers to the number of daisies in a garden is $4 : 9$. What fraction of the sunflowers are daisies?

Ans: _____

22. The number of pens and pencils in a box is in the ratio $4 : 7$. How many times as many pencils as pens are there?

Ans: _____

23. John's savings is $\frac{8}{9}$ of May's savings. What is the ratio of John's savings to May's savings to their total savings?

Ans: _____

24. Byron adds 2 cups of syrup for every 7 cups of juice to make a drink. How many cups of syrup does he need for 35 cups of juice?

Ans: _____ cups

25. A pot contained 6 liters of soup. Sophie poured all
of it equally into some bowls. If each bowl had
$\frac{3}{8}$ liter of soup, how many bowls did she fill?

Ans: _____ bowls

26. Each box of cornflakes contains $3q$ stickers. Gemma
bought 6 boxes and gave 5 of the stickers away.
How many stickers did she have left?
Give your answer in terms of q.

Ans: _____ stickers

27. Zoe drank $150j$ milliliters of milk. Jay drank a third
of what Zoe drank and Kerry drank 73 milliliters
more than Jay. How much milk did Kerry drink?
Give your answer in terms of j.

Ans: _____ mL

28. There were 40 visitors to an art gallery on Monday.
On Tuesday, there were 24 visitors.
What is the percentage decrease in the visitors?

Ans: _____%

29. The number of adults and children at a fair are in the
ratio 10 : 3. If there were 143 people at the fair, how
many more adults than children were there?

Ans: _____ adults

30. If 35% of a number is 343, what is 50% of the number?

Ans: _____

31. A grapefruit is $\frac{3}{10}$ as heavy as a watermelon. If the watermelon has a mass of 950 grams, what is the mass of the grapefruit?

Ans: _____ g

32. Suria scored 60% on a test. If she scored 36 points, what was the total score for the test?

Ans: _____ points

33. Five girls are standing in line at an ice cream shop.
Rita is standing in front of Mary Jo and behind Sue.
Lin is standing behind Beth but in front of Sue.
Who is the first in the line?

Ans: _____

34. How many triangular faces does the solid below have?

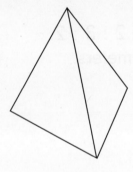

Ans: _____ triangular faces

35. What two shapes are the faces of the solid below?

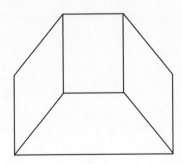

Ans: _____

25

Section C

For questions 36 to 45, each answer carries 1 point.
Write your answer in the space provided.
Show your work.

36. The isosceles triangle XYZ below is not drawn to scale.

   a. Express the perimeter of the triangle in terms of a.
   b. If $a = 6$ centimeters, what is the area of the triangle?

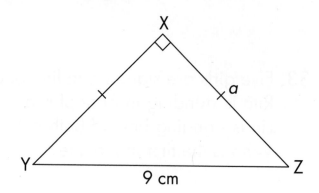

37. The sides of Triangle DEF are in the ratio 2 : 3 : 2.
    The perimeter of the triangle is 133 centimeters.
    What is the length of its longest side?

38. A box contains 8 orange cubes, 11 green cubes,
7 blue cubes, and 4 black cubes. Anton draws a cube
at random from the box.

a. What is the probability of drawing a green cube or
a black cube?

b. He doubles the number of black cubes in the box.
What is the probability of drawing an orange
cube or a black cube?

39. A gift box contains *v* crayons and 5 markers. Osman buys 12 boxes and repacks the crayons and markers equally into 6 boxes.

    a. How many crayons and markers does he have in all?

    b. How many crayons and markers will there be in each box now?

40. The number of students in a club in March was 120. In May, the number decreased by 15%. By December, the number increased by 50%. How many students were there in the club by December?

41. There are $\frac{3}{7}$ as many craft books as travel guides on a bookshelf. There are 550 books in all.

    a. How many travel guides are there?
    b. 110 more craft books are added to the bookshelf. What is the ratio of the number of craft books to the number of travel guides?

42. In the figure below, not drawn to scale, WXYZ is a rhombus. Find the measure of:

    a. ∠XWZ
    b. ∠XVZ

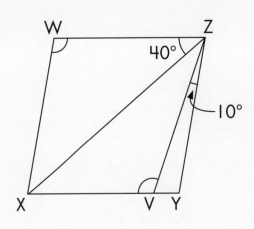

43. $\frac{3}{4}$ of Benny's stamp collection is equal to $\frac{5}{6}$ of Clay's stamp collection. Benny has 20 more stamps than Clay. How many stamps do they have in all?

44. A bakery sold 3 kinds of pies last week. The number of cherry pies and pecan pies sold were in the ratio 7 : 9. The number of pecan pies and key lime pies sold were in the ratio 3 : 1. If 90 key lime pies were sold, how many cherry pies and pecan pies were sold in all?

45. 55% of the audience in a theater was boys.
During the intermission, 20% of the girls left.
There were 864 girls left in the theater. How many
boys and girls were there at first?

Mid-Year Test C

Section A

Questions 1 to 15 carry 1 point each. For each question, choose the correct answer and write its letter in the parentheses provided.

1. Simplify $12 + n - 8n$.
    a. $12 + 7n$
    b. $4 + 8n$
    c. $12 - 7n$
    d. $4 + n$ (   )

2. If $g = 3$, find $7g + 2g + 3$.
    a. 30   b. 26
    c. 12   d. 9   (   )

3. What number does y represent?

    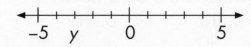

    a. 3   b. –1
    c. –2   d. –3   (   )

Use the table below to answer questions 4 and 5.

Greta fills a bag with some colored gumballs and picks one at random.

Color	Number of Gumballs
Red	10
Yellow	4
Green	6
Purple	5
White	5

4. What color is she most likely to pick?
    a. red   b. yellow
    c. green   d. white   (   )

5. What is the probability that she will pick a purple gumball?
    a. $\frac{1}{4}$ b. $\frac{1}{5}$
    c. $\frac{1}{6}$ d. $\frac{3}{10}$ (   )

6. The rectangle below is not drawn to scale. Find the measure of ∠a.

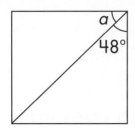

   a. 32°   b. 42°
   c. 132°   d. 138°   (   )

7. Name the solid formed by this net.

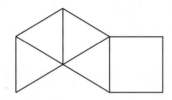

   a. pyramid   b. cuboid
   c. prism   d. cone   (   )

8. Which solid below has 3 faces?

a.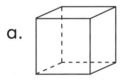

b.

c.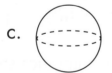

d.

                                  (   )

9. There are 4 liters of water in a jug. Intan drinks $\frac{2}{3}$ liter of the water every hour. How many hours will she take to finish the water?

   a. 2   b. 3
   c. 6   d. 8

10. Prema, Jarod, and Rosie shared some paper clips in the ratio 3 : 5 : 2. What fraction of the total number of paper clips did Jarod receive?

   a. $\frac{1}{2}$ b. $\frac{3}{5}$

   c. $\frac{5}{8}$ d. $\frac{2}{3}$ (   )

11. Sara had 6 times as many pretzels as Ken. If they had 56 pretzels in all, how many pretzels did Sara have?

   a. 48   b. 49
   c. 50   d. 54   (   )

12. Which number line below shows 3 – 5?

a.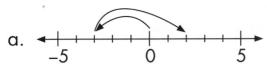

b.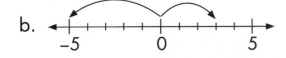

c.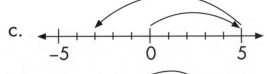

d.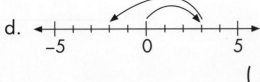

( )

13. A deli offers 5 kinds of sandwich meats, 2 kinds of cheese, and 3 kinds of breads.

Deli Sandwiches		
Meats	Cheeses	Breads
5	2	3

How many different combinations of 1 meat, 1 cheese, and 1 bread can be made?
a. 10   b. 15
c. 24   d. 30   ( )

14. 5 cars of different colors lined up at the traffic light. A red car is in front of a blue car but behind a green one. A black car is behind a white one but in front of the green car. What color is the car that is last in line?
a. red   b. green
c. black   d. blue   ( )

15. Keri's class planted 30% of the plants around the school. What information do you need to find out how many plants her class had planted?
a. the number of plants planted by each student in Keri's class
b. the total number of plants planted in the school
c. the number of students in the school
d. the number of seeds needed   ( )

Section B

For questions 16 to 35, each answer carries 1 point.
Write your answer in the answer blank provided.

16. Name the solid formed by this net.

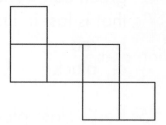

Ans: _____

17. What number does *z* represent?

Ans: _____

18. Trapezoid EFGH below is not drawn to scale.
    What is the measure of ∠FEH?

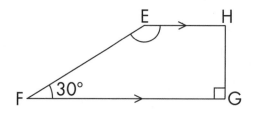

Ans: _____°

19. What is the value of $6m + 5 - 2m + 3$ when $m = 7$?

Ans: _____

20. The ratio of the number of goldfish to the number of guppies in a bowl is 7 : 5. How many times as many goldfish as guppies are there?

Ans: _____

21. The ratio of the number of adults to the number of children on a train is 5 : 3. What fraction of the total number of passengers are children?

Ans: _____

22. A baker used $\frac{1}{3}$ liter of milk together with $\frac{1}{2}$ liter of honey in a recipe. What is the ratio of the amount of milk to the amount of honey used in the recipe?

Ans: _____

23. An empty bowl has a mass of c grams. Dana puts 200 grams of beans in each bowl. Express the mass of 12 such bowls in terms of c.

Ans: _____ g

24. Rekha's mass is $16p$ kilograms. Her mass is half that of Doug while Baron is 11 kilograms lighter than Doug. What is Baron's mass in terms of p?

Ans: _____ kg

25. Ashley has $\frac{2}{3}$ as many red marbles as green marbles. If he has 22 red marbles, how many green marbles does he have?

Ans: _____ marbles

26. The number of tulips to lilies at the florist's are in the ratio of 5 : 6. If there are 72 lilies, how many flowers are there in all?

Ans: _____ flowers

27. A wooden beam is $\frac{3}{4}$ meter long. Charlie cuts it into smaller blocks, each measuring $\frac{1}{8}$ meter long. How many blocks are there?

Ans: _____ blocks

28. In 2011, there were 18 295 students enrolled in a school. In 2012, the number increased to 20 100. What is the percentage increase in the enrolment? Give your answer to the nearest percent.

Ans: _____%

29. If 60% of a number is 594, what is $\frac{1}{6}$ of that number?

Ans: _____

30. Putra placed some counters in 3 boxes. He placed 3 times as many counters in Box A than in Box B. The number of counters in Box C was a quarter of the total in Box A and Box B. What is the ratio of the number of counters in Box A to Box B to Box C?

Ans: _____

31. Alicia had a book of stickers. 25% are animal stickers, 30% are doll stickers, and the remainder are alphabet stickers. What is the ratio of the number of alphabet stickers to the total number of stickers?

Ans: _____

32. Evra rolls a six-sided die numbered 1 to 6 on its sides. What is the probability of him rolling an even number greater than 3?

Ans: _____

33. A container holds 3 red balls, 2 orange balls, 5 yellow balls, and 3 green balls. A ball is picked at random. What is the probability of choosing neither red nor green?

Ans: _____

34. The figure below is not drawn to scale. STUW is a parallelogram. WUV is an equilateral triangle and TUV is a straight line. Find the measure of ∠STU.

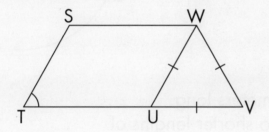

Ans: _____°

35. How many rectangular faces does the solid below have?

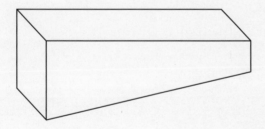

Ans: _____ rectangular faces

Section C

For questions 36 to 45, each answer carries 1 point.
Write your answer in the space provided.
Show your work.

36. The figure below is not drawn to scale. O is the center of the circle. Find the measure of

    a. ∠ORP
    b. ∠QRO

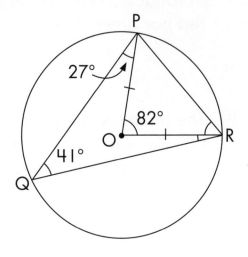

37. A piece of fabric measures 128 meters long.
    Husain wants to cut the fabric into shorter lengths of
    $\frac{5}{12}$ meter each.

    a. How many shorter lengths can he cut from the fabric?
    b. What is the length of fabric that will be left over?

38. Kay had 100 beads. Louise had $\frac{11}{20}$ the number of Kay's beads. Kay used up 60% of her beads and gave 10% of the remainder to Louise. How many beads did Louise have in the end?

39. There are 8 green buttons, 3 blue buttons, 5 purple buttons, and 2 black buttons in a box. Elva picks a button at random.

   a. What is the probability of choosing a button that is not purple?
   b. If she takes out all the green buttons then picks a button at random, what is the probability of choosing a button that is not blue?

40. The ratio of the number of roses to carnations in a garden is 3 : 8. The ratio of the number of tulips to roses in the garden is 5 : 6. If there are 462 carnations and tulips together, how many roses are there?

41. Diya read $\frac{1}{6}$ of a book on Sunday. She read $\frac{1}{2}$ of the remaining pages on Wednesday and finished reading the last 60 pages on Thursday.

   a. How many pages did she read on Sunday?
   b. How many pages were there in the book?

42. A bookend and a notepad have a mass of 600 grams.
The mass of 8 bookends and 5 notepads is 4200 grams.
What is the mass of each bookend?

43. $\frac{5}{6}$ of the number of girls in a class is equal to $\frac{2}{3}$ of the
number of boys. If there are 36 students in the class,
how many girls are there?

44. The ratio of the number of white eggs to brown eggs in a tray was 5 : 8. Jack added 60% more white eggs and 50% more brown eggs. What percentage of the eggs are brown?

45. A square plot of land of sides d metres requires the same length of fencing as a rectangular plot of land.

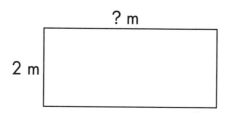

? m

2 m

a. Express the length of the rectangular plot of land in terms of d.

b. If $d = 8$, what is the area of the rectangular plot?

Mid-Year Test D

Section A

Questions 1 to 15 carry 1 point each. For each question, choose the correct answer and write its letter in the parentheses provided.

1. Simplify $8z - 12 + 3z$.
    a. $3z - 4$
    b. $11z - 12$
    c. $8z - 9$
    d. $20z + 3$ ( )

2. If $k = 3$, what is the value of $15k - 8 + 2k$?
    a. 9   b. 11
    c. 39   d. 43   ( )

3. What number is the arrow pointing at?

    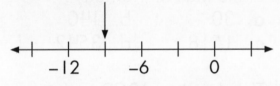

    a. −7   b. −8
    c. −9   d. −10   ( )

4. How many thirds are there in 8?
    a. 3   b. 8
    c. 16   d. 24   ( )

5. The triangle below is not drawn to scale. Find the measure of $\angle z$.

    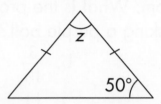

    a. 50°   b. 80°
    c. 100°   d. 230°   ( )

6. Which solid below has 5 faces?
    a.

    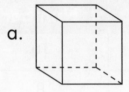

    b.

    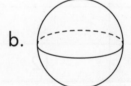

    c.

    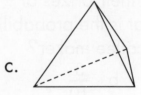

    d.

    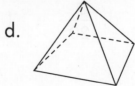

                                    ( )

7. The heights of Eric, Nicole, and Amelia are in the ratio 4 : 5 : 3. What fraction of their total height is Nicole's height?

a. $\frac{5}{12}$ b. $\frac{1}{2}$

c. $\frac{5}{7}$ d. $\frac{4}{5}$ ( )

8. There are 9 red balls, 6 pink balls, 10 yellow balls, 6 purple balls, and 11 white balls in a pouch. Indra picks a ball at random. What is the probability of picking a purple ball?

a. $\frac{1}{7}$ b. $\frac{3}{14}$

c. $\frac{5}{21}$ d. $\frac{11}{42}$ ( )

9. A lucky draw offers the prizes below.

Prizes	Number
Toaster	14
Iron	8
Sandwich Maker	6
Coffee Maker	12

Winners pick their prizes at random. What is the probability of picking a coffee maker?

a. $\frac{1}{5}$ b. $\frac{3}{10}$

c. $\frac{3}{20}$ d. $\frac{7}{20}$ ( )

10. There are 4 times as many adults as children on a cruise ship. If there were 3140 people on board, how many children are there?

a. 628   b. 785

c. 1705   d. 2512   ( )

11. 35% of the books collected for a charity were donated by a school. The other donations provided 52 000 books. How many books did the school donate?

a. 800

b. 18 200

c. 28 000

d. 80 000   ( )

12. The number of people in a mall on Sunday was 2530. On Monday, the number decreased by 40%. How many people were at the mall on Monday?

a. 30   b. 140

c. 1518   d. 3542   ( )

13. The rhombus ABCD is not drawn to scale. What is the measure of ∠ABD?

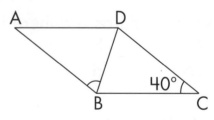

a. 40°   b. 70°

c. 140°   d. 180°   ( )

14. What does the number line show?

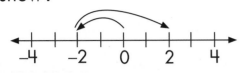

a. 2 − 2
b. 2 + 2
c. −2 + 4
d. 1 − 2 + 2   ( )

15. A funfair booth offers winners a choice from each of the 3 categories below.

Soft Toys	Board Games	Card Games
3	4	3

How many different combinations of 1 soft toy, 1 board game, and 1 card game is there?
a. 10   b. 21
c. 24   d. 36   ( )

Section B

For questions 16 to 35, each answer carries 1 point.
Write your answer in the answer blank provided.

16. What number does y represent?

Ans: _____

17. If $h = 5$, find the value of $10h + 7 − 3h − 4$.

Ans: _____

18. Name the solid formed by this net.

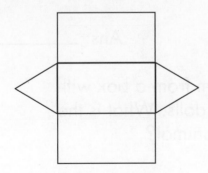

Ans: _____

19. The ratio of the number of scarves to belts in a drawer is 2 : 4. How many times as many belts as scarves are there?

Ans: _____

20. The ratio of the number of buns to the number of hotdogs at a hotdog stand is 9 : 6. What fraction of the buns are the hotdogs?

Ans: _____

21. Anna has $\frac{5}{11}$ as many magnets as Martha. What is the ratio of the number of magnets Anna has to the total number of magnets?

Ans: _____

22. Sunita had $2w$ postcards. Her sister had 8 times as many postcards while her brother had 5 less than her sister. How many postcards did Sunita's brother have?

Ans: _____ postcards

23. Grace gave each of her classmates $3t$ cookies and had 10 left over. How many cookies did she have at first if she had 36 classmates? Give your answer in terms of t.

Ans: _____ cookies

24. Dewi wanted to pick a toy at random from a box with 6 stuffed animals, 7 puzzles, and 3 dolls. What is the probability of her picking a stuffed animal?

Ans: _____

25. Lisa had 12 kilograms of beans. She packed them into smaller packs each with a mass of $\frac{4}{5}$ kilogram. How many smaller packets will she have?

Ans: _____ packets

26. Cara had $\frac{2}{9}$ as many daisies as carnations. If she has 153 carnations, how many daisies does she have?

Ans: _____ daisies

27. Rectangle PQRS is not drawn to scale. Find the measure of ∠PTR.

Ans: _____ °

28. 40% of the participants in a contest were ladies. If there were 240 ladies, how many people participated in the contest?

Ans: _____ people

29. Lily scored 60 points for her first math test. She scored 85 points for her second math test. What is the percentage increase in her score?

Ans: _____%

30. 40% of a number is 600. What is 85% of the same number?

Ans: _____

31. $\frac{1}{5}$ of a group of students come to school by train and
$\frac{2}{3}$ by bus. An equal number of the rest of the students
cycle, walk, or travel by car. What fraction of the
students walk to school?

Ans: _____

32. The number of blue beads and white beads in a box
are in the ratio 3 : 7. If there are 196 white beads,
how many more white beads than blue beads are there?

Ans: _____ white beads

33. Five students sat in a row of seats. Bruce sat on one end.
Grace sat between Bruce and Miles. Rita sat between
Miles and Chad. Who sat in the middle seat?

Ans: _____

34. How many triangular faces does the solid below have?

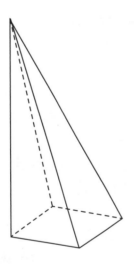

Ans: _____ triangular faces

35. What two shapes are the faces of the solid below?

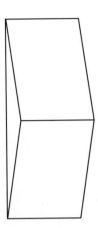

Ans: _____

Section C

**For questions 36 to 45, each answer carries 1 point.
Write your answer in the space provided.
Show your work.**

36. At a concert, there were $\frac{2}{3}$ as many women as men.
    There were 9u men.

    a. How many women were there?
    b. How many people were there in all?

37. The length of a carpet is 4 times its width.
Its width is x centimeters long.

    a. What is the perimeter of the carpet?
    b. If $x = 28$, what is its area?

38. Mina had $4\frac{2}{3}$ meters of ribbon. She used $1\frac{3}{4}$ meters for her classroom display board and $2\frac{1}{2}$ meters for wrapping presents. She divided the remainder equally to make 3 brooches. How much ribbon did she use for each brooch?

39. Ishak placed 4 silver bells, 7 pink bells, 3 purple bells, and 5 blue bells in a bag. He picks a bell from the bag at random.

    a. What is the probability of him picking a bell that is not pink?

    b. If he doubles the number of blue bells, what is the new probability of picking a bell that is not pink?

40. A factory makes $\frac{5}{9}$ as many pouches as backpacks in a month. 1944 backpacks were made.

    a. How many more backpacks than pouches were made?

    b. How many pouches are made in a year?

41. A store sold imported teas from China and India in the ratio 5 : 4. Teas from Kenya and India are in the ratio 5 : 6. There were 1290 boxes of tea imported from China.

   a. From which country did the store import the greatest number of boxes?

   b. How many boxes of tea did the store import in all?

42. A bus and a van can carry a total of 72 children.
    4 buses and 3 vans can carry a total of 276 children.
    How many children can each bus carry?

43. The ratio of the number of daisies to the number of lilies
    in a garden is 6 : 5. After more flowers were planted,
    the number of daisies increased by 25% and the
    number of lilies increased by 20%. What is the ratio of the
    number of daisies to the number of lilies now?

44. At a party, 40% of the guests were male. 25% of the
    female guests were adults and the remainder
    180 were girls. How many guests were there at
    the party?

45. $\frac{5}{8}$ of the apples in a crate is equal to $\frac{2}{5}$ of the oranges
    in the crate. There are 45 more oranges than apples.
    How many apples and oranges are there in all?

End-of-Year Test E

Section A

Questions 1 to 15 carry 1 point each. For each question, choose the correct answer and write its letter in the parentheses provided.

1. If $k = 5$, what is the value of $7k + 4k - 13$?
   a. 10   b. 11
   c. 24   d. 42   ( )

2. This chart shows the average winter temperature over four days.

Day	Average Temperature
Sunday	−6°C
Monday	0°C
Tuesday	−4°C
Wednesday	6°C

   Which day had the lowest average temperature?
   a. Sunday
   b. Monday
   c. Tuesday
   d. Wednesday   ( )

This pie chart shows the types of movies available at a movie rental store. Use the chart to answer questions 3 and 4.

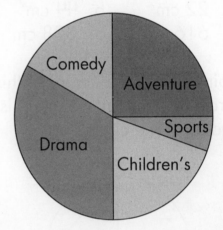

3. The store has a total of 1000 movies. About how many are adventure movies?
   a. 100   b. 250
   c. 500   d. 800   ( )

4. Which category has the most movies?
   a. Sports   b. Comedy
   c. Children's   d. Drama   ( )

5. How many fifths are there in 5 wholes?
   a. 1   b. 5
   c. 10   d. 25   (   )

6. Find the area of the circle.
   $$\left(\text{Take } \pi = \frac{22}{7}\right)$$

   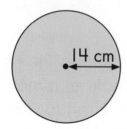

   14 cm

   a. 22 cm^2 b. 44 cm^2
   c. 616 cm^2 d. 308 cm^2 (   )

7. Point O is at the center of this circle. Which line segment is a radius of the circle?

   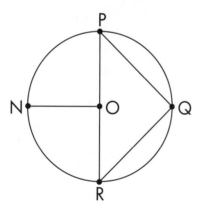

   a. $\overline{NO}$ b. $\overline{QR}$
   c. $\overline{PQ}$ d. $\overline{PR}$ (   )

8. A total of 200 raffle tickets have been sold, and 50 of those tickets will win prizes. If you have only one raffle ticket, what are the chances that you will win a prize?
   a. 1 in 3   b. 1 in 4
   c. 1 in 5   d. 1 in 6   (   )

9. Eva, Raihan, and Sunita shared a box of clay in the ratio 3 : 6 : 5. What fraction of the box of clay did Raihan get?
   a. $\frac{3}{14}$ b. $\frac{5}{14}$

   c. $\frac{3}{7}$ d. $\frac{1}{2}$ (   )

10. Melissa bought 6 kilograms of rice. She used $\frac{3}{4}$ kilogram of rice every day. How many days did she take to finish the rice?
    a. 8 days   b. 4.5 days
    c. 4 days   d. 3 days   (   )

11. Town A and Town B are 40 kilometers apart. If Drew drove at a speed of 60 kilometers per hour, how long did she take to drive from Town A to Town B?
    a. $\frac{2}{5}$ h   b. $\frac{2}{3}$ h

    c. $\frac{1}{3}$ h   d. $\frac{1}{2}$ h   (   )

12. Azman took 15 minutes to jog from his home to his school. If he jogged at a speed of 10 kilometers per hour, how far was his school from his home?
   a. 40 km   b. 25 km
   c. 2.5 km   d. 5 km   (   )

13. The figure shows a square with an area of 100 square centimeters and a semicircle. Find the perimeter of the figure. (Take $\pi = 3.14$)

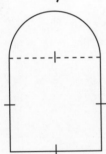

   a. 45.7 cm   b. 30 cm
   c. 15.7 cm   d. 14.3 cm (   )

14. The figure shows a semicircle and a quadrant. Find the perimeter of the figure. $\left(\text{Take } \pi = \dfrac{22}{7}\right)$

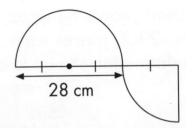

28 cm

   a. 66 cm   b. 94 cm
   c. 108 cm   d. 122 cm (   )

15. Zoe rolls two number cubes numbered 1–6. What is the probability that she will roll 10 on one try?
   a. $\dfrac{3}{35}$ b. $\dfrac{1}{12}$

   c. $\dfrac{1}{10}$ d. $\dfrac{4}{9}$ (   )

Section B

For questions 16 to 35, each answer carries 1 point.
Write your answer in the answer blank provided.

The pie chart shows the types of bread sold by a bakery
in a week. 2400 pieces were sold altogether.
Use the information shown to answer questions 16, 17, and 18.

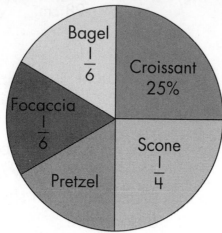

16. How many scones were sold?

Ans: _____ scones

17. How many more croissants than bagels were sold?

Ans: _____ croissants

18. How many pretzels were sold?

Ans: _____ pretzels

19. There were 50 students in the school choir.
    30% of them were girls. How many boys were there?

Ans: _____ boys

20. The number of boys in a hall are $\frac{3}{4}$ the number of girls.
    How many children are there if there are 42 boys in the hall?

Ans: _____ children

21. Mrs Thatcher gave $5s$ marbles to each student in her class. She had 7 marbles left. How many marbles did she have at first if she had 40 students? Give your answer in terms of s.

Ans: _____ marbles

22. Bus A had 70 passengers while Bus B had 56 passengers. How many percent more passengers were there in Bus A than in Bus B?

Ans: _____%

23. Amit is driving a van at a speed of 52 kilometers per hour. At this speed, how far would he travel in 3.5 hours?

Ans: _____ km

24. A cyclist can travel 4.5 kilometers in 45 minutes. What is his speed?

Ans: _____ km/h

25. Brenda drove 60 kilometers in 40 minutes and continued driving 42 kilometers in 45 minutes. What was her average speed?

Ans: _____ km/h

26. Find the capacity of a tank measuring 67 centimeters by 40 centimeters by 20 centimeters. Express your answer in liters. ($1 L = 1000 cm^3$)

Ans: _____ L

27. A rectangular tank 70 centimeters by 30 centimeters by 40 centimeters is $\frac{3}{4}$-filled with water. How much water is in the tank? Express your answer in liters. ($1 L = 1000 cm^3$)

Ans: _____ L

28. The volume of a plank of wood is 96 000 cubic centimeters.
    The area of its base is 3200 square centimeters.
    What is the height of the plank of wood?

    Ans: _____ cm

29. Laila, Cheryl, and Sheena sold 325 funfair tickets
    altogether. Laila sold $\frac{1}{3}$ as many tickets as Cheryl
    while Cheryl sold $\frac{1}{3}$ as many as tickets as Sheena.
    How many tickets did Laila sell?

    Ans: _____ tickets

30. The figure is made up of four identical triangles.
    Find the area of the shaded part of the figure.

    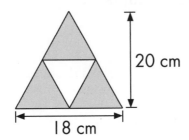

    20 cm

    18 cm

    Ans: _____ cm^2

31. The figure shows a quadrant and a semicircle.
    Find the area of the unshaded part of the figure.
    $\left(\text{Take } \pi = \frac{22}{7} \right)$

    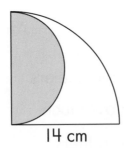

    14 cm

    Ans: _____ cm^2

32. The figure shows a semicircle and two quadrants of radius 7 centimeters. Find the perimeter of the shaded part of the figure. $\left(\text{Take } \pi = \dfrac{22}{7} \right)$

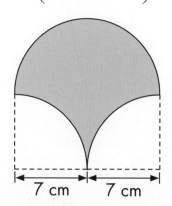

7 cm   7 cm

Ans: _____ cm

33. The figure shows the net of a cube. If the shaded square is the top of the cube, which face is the base of the cube?

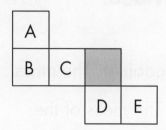

A		
B	C	
	D	E

Ans: _____

34. The figure shows an equilateral triangle and a semicircle. Find the perimeter of the figure. $\left(\text{Take } \pi = \dfrac{22}{7} \right)$

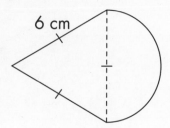

6 cm

Ans: _____ cm

35. Find the area of the figure below.

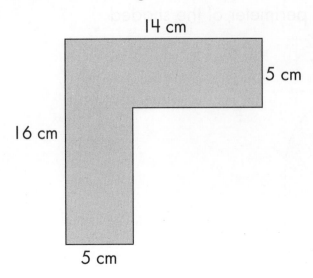

14 cm

5 cm

16 cm

5 cm

Ans: _____ cm²

Section C

For questions 36 to 45, each answer carries 1 point.
Write your answer in the space provided.
Show your work.

36. The mass of a table is $\frac{5}{6}$ the mass of a cabinet. The mass

    of a stool is $\frac{1}{4}$ the mass of the cabinet. The mass of the

    stool is 4.5 kilograms.

    a. Find the ratio of the mass of the table to the mass of
       the cabinet to the mass of the stool.
    b. What is the average mass of the three pieces of
       furniture?

37. A car left Town A for Town B at 10.25 a.m. For the first 30 minutes, the car traveled at an average speed of 80 kilometers per hour. It then traveled at an average speed of 75 kilometers per hour for the next 2 hours to reach Town B.

   a. Find the distance from Town A to Town B.
   b. At what time did the car reach Town B?

38. The figure shows 4 identical circles in a square. Find the area of the unshaded part of the figure.

   $$\left(\text{Take } \pi = \frac{22}{7} \right)$$

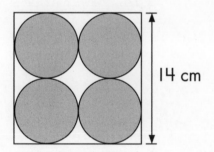

14 cm

39. A container 24 centimeters long, 10 centimeters wide, and 40 centimeters high is $\frac{1}{4}$-filled with water. Another 400 cubic centimeters of water are then added to the container. How many liters of water are in the container in the end? (1 L = 1000 cm^3)

40. The cuboid and cube shown have the same volume. Find the length of one edge of the cube.

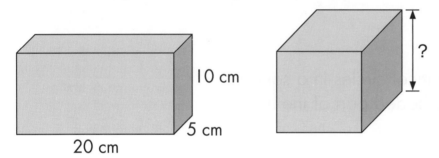

10 cm

5 cm

20 cm

?

41. A cubical container has a capacity of 0.512 liters. What is the area of the base? (1 L = 1000 cm^3)

42. Nisha poured 1.32 liters of water into an empty
    container 22 centimeters long, 15 centimeters wide,
    and 10 centimeters high.

    a. What is the height of the water level?
    b. How many liters of water are needed to fill the
       container to the brim? (1 L = 1000 cm^3)

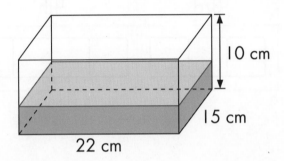

43. Joseph drove at an average speed of 80 kilometers
    per hour from his house to his office which is
    120 kilometers away.

    a. How long did it take Joseph to reach his office?
    b. At what speed must he drive to reach his office
       15 minutes earlier?

44. Liam is forming a pattern with toothpicks.

   a. How many toothpicks does he need to form the 12th figure?
   b. How many toothpicks does he need to form the 24th figure?

Figure	1st	2nd	3rd	4th
Pattern	▢	▢▢	▢▢▢	▢▢▢▢

45. The figure shows a square of side 4 centimeters, a smaller square of side 2 centimeters, and 2 quadrants. Find the area of the unshaded part. (Take π = 3.14)

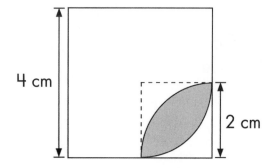

4 cm

2 cm

End-of-Year Test F

Section A

Questions 1 to 15 carry 1 point each. For each question, choose the correct answer and write its letter in the parentheses provided.

1. Simplify $8 - 5j - 3 + 4j$.
    a. $3 + j$ b. $5 - j$
    c. $5 + 9j$ d. $2 + 4j$ (   )

2. What number is the arrow pointing at?

    a. -160 b. -140
    c. -120 d. -40 (   )

This pie chart shows the types of games at a funfair. Use the chart to answer questions 3 and 4.

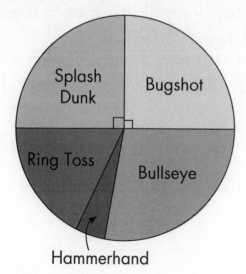

Hammerhand

3. 2000 people visited the funfair. Each of them played one game. How many people played Splash Dunk and Bugshot?
    a. 50   b. 388
    c. 500   d. 1000   (   )

4. Which was the most popular game?
    a. Bullseye
    b. Splash Dunk
    c. Bugshot
    d. Ring Toss   (   )

5. Point C is at the center of this circle. Which line segment is the diameter of the circle?

    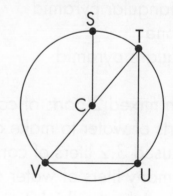

    a. $\overline{SC}$ b. $\overline{TU}$
    c. $\overline{CV}$ d. $\overline{VT}$ (   )

6. Find the circumference of the circle. $\left(\text{Take } \pi = \dfrac{22}{7}\right)$

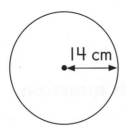

14 cm

   a. 22 cm
   b. 26 cm
   c. 44 cm
   d. 88 cm   (   )

7. Find the area of the semicircle. $\left(\text{Take } \pi = \dfrac{22}{7}\right)$

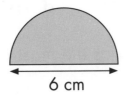

6 cm

   a. $9\dfrac{3}{7}$ cm^2
   b. $14\dfrac{1}{7}$ cm^2
   c. $18\dfrac{6}{7}$ cm^2
   d. $28\dfrac{2}{7}$ cm^2 (   )

8. Which of these solids has five faces?
   a. cube
   b. triangular pyramid
   c. cone
   d. square pyramid   (   )

9. Johan mixed 2 parts of cordial to 5 parts of water to make a drink. If he used 3.2 liters of cordial, how many liters of water did he use to make the drink?
   a. 25 L
   b. 16 L
   c. 10 L
   d. 8 L   (   )

10. Patrick made 36 puppets for sale. If this is 45% of the total number of puppets he wants to make, how many puppets does he want to make in all?
    a. 80
    b. 72
    c. 65
    d. 45   (   )

11. The mass of a dictionary is 7 times that of a notebook. If their total mass is 2 kilograms, what is the difference in their masses?
    a. 250 g
    b. 285 g
    c. 1500 g
    d. 1750 g   (   )

12. Arthur cycled from Point A to Point B at an average speed of 12 kilometers per hour. He took 45 minutes to reach Point B. How far did he cycle?
    a. 8 km
    b. 9 km
    c. 12 km
    d. 45 km   (   )

13. Tim drove from Town X to Town Y which is 80 kilometers away at an average speed of 100 kilometers per hour. How long did he take to reach Town Y?
    a. 48 min
    b. 45 min
    c. 35 min
    d. 10 min   (   )

14. The figure shows two circles. Find the area of the shaded part. (Take π = 3.14)

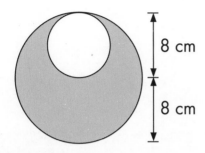

8 cm

8 cm

   a. 75.36 cm²
   b. 100.5 cm²
   c. 150.72 cm²
   d. 200.96 cm²   (   )

15. The figure shows a rectangle and a semicircle.
The area of the rectangle is 200 square centimeters. What is the perimeter of the figure? (Take π = 3.14)

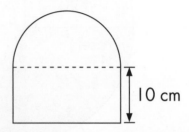

10 cm

   a. 40 cm   b. 71.4 cm
   c. 31.4 cm   d. 197 cm (   )

Section B

For questions 16 to 35, each answer carries 1 point.
Write your answer in the answer blank provided.

16. The length of a spade is $\frac{2}{7}$ of the length of a rake.

What is the ratio of the length of the spade to that of the rake to their total length?

Ans: _____

17. I mixed $\frac{1}{4}$ kilogram of flour with $\frac{1}{8}$ kilogram of butter.

What is the ratio of the amount of butter to the amount of flour I used?

Ans: _____

18. Gina takes 7 minutes to paint a clay model. How many such models can she paint in 1 hour 3 minutes?

Ans: _____ models

71

The pie chart shows the number of items collected by Abby.
Use the information shown to answer questions 19, 20, and 21.

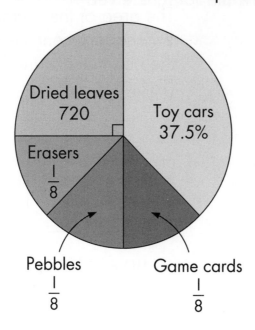

19. How many pebbles did Abby collect?

Ans: _____ pebbles

20. What is the total number of items Abby collected?

Ans: _____ items

21. How many game cards and erasers did Abby
collect in all?

Ans: _____

22. A jug holds *v* liters of water. The jug holds 3 times
as much water as a beaker. A pot holds 10 times as
much water as the jug. How much water is there in all?

Ans: _____ L

23. If 28% of a number is 336, what is 60% of that number?

Ans: _____

24. Raj, John, and Fern shared 198 tokens at a carnival.
Raj got $\frac{1}{2}$ as many tokens as John while John received
$\frac{1}{4}$ as many tokens as Fern. How many tokens did Raj get?

Ans: _____ tokens

25. The capacity of a cubical box is 343 cubic centimeters.
Find the length of each edge of the box.

Ans: _____ cm

26. A go-kart driver travels 45 kilometers in 40 minutes.
What is his speed?

Ans: _____ km/h

27. Lester drove 110 kilometers in an hour and continued
driving another 100 kilometers in 1 hour 20 minutes.
What was his average speed?

Ans: _____ km/h

28. A cardboard box with a square base of length
9 centimeters has a height of 21 centimeters.
Find the volume of the cardboard box.

Ans: _____ cm^3

29. A rectangular aquarium with a base measuring
85 centimeters by 50 centimeters is filled to a depth
of 10 centimeters with water. How much water is in
the tank? Express your answer in liters. (1 L = 1000 cm^3)

Ans: _____ L

30. A tank measuring 76 centimeters by 45 centimeters by 40 centimeters is half-filled with water. How many liters of water are there in the tank? (1 L = 1000 cm³)

Ans: _____ L

31. The figure shows a small semicircle and a larger semicircle. Find the area of the unshaded part of the figure. $\left(\text{Take } \pi = \dfrac{22}{7}\right)$

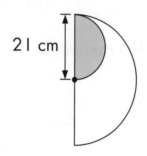

21 cm

Ans: _____ cm²

32. Shawn has a semicircular piece of cardboard. He cuts out a smaller semicircle as shown. Find the perimeter of the remaining piece of cardboard. $\left(\text{Take } \pi = \dfrac{22}{7}\right)$

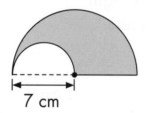

7 cm

Ans: _____ cm

33. The figure shows a semicircle and two quadrants. Find the perimeter of the figure. (Take π = 3.14)

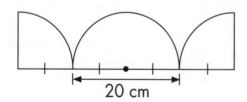

20 cm

Ans: _____ cm

34. The figure shows the net of a cube. If the shaded square is the bottom of the cube, which face is the top of the cube?

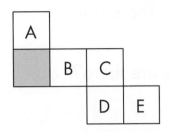

Ans: _____

35. The figure is made up of a square and two identical triangles. The perimeter of the square is 36 centimeters. What is the total area of the two triangles?

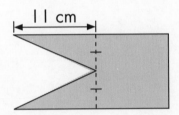

Ans: _____ cm²

Section C

For questions 36 to 45, each answer carries 1 point.
Write your answer in the space provided.
Show your work.

36. Pia has a roll of cloth measuring 29 meters in length. She wants to cut it into shorter strips each measuring $\frac{4}{7}$ meter long.

   a. How many strips can she cut from the roll of cloth?
   b. What is the length of cloth left over?

75

37. The ratio of the number of apples to the number of plums at a grocery store is 3 : 8. The ratio of the number of lemons to the number of plums is 3 : 2. There are 84 lemons.

   a. How many more plums than apples are there?
   b. How many fruits are there in all?

38. A truck left Town A for Town B. For the first 1 hour 10 minutes, the truck traveled at an average speed of 70 kilometers per hour. For the next 40 minutes, it traveled at an average speed of 50 kilometers per hour before reaching Town B. How far apart are Town A and Town B?

39. The figure shows 4 identical quadrants in a square.
    Find the area of the unshaded part of the figure.
    $\left(\text{Take } \pi = \dfrac{22}{7}\right)$

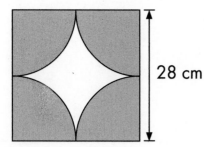

28 cm

40. A container 32 centimeters long, 20 centimeters wide,
    and 40 centimeters high is $\dfrac{1}{4}$-filled with water.

    Then, 600 cubic centimeters of water are poured out.
    How many liters of water are left in the container?
    $(1 \text{ L} = 1000 \text{ cm}^3)$

41. The figure shows a circle of radius 8 meters. Find the area of the shaded part. (Take $\pi = 3.14$)

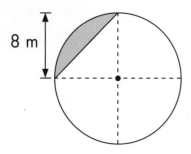

8 m

42. A rectangular container with length 9 centimeters and breadth 6 centimeters is full of water. All the water can be used to fill 2 cubical containers of edge 6 centimeters to the brim.

    a. How much water was in the rectangular container?
    b. What is the height of the rectangular container?

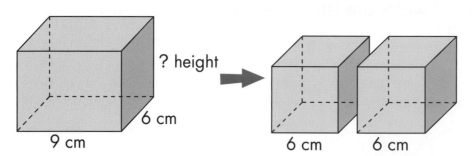

? height

9 cm   6 cm   6 cm   6 cm

43. Brenda drove at an average speed of 75 kilometers per hour from her home to the ferry terminal 175 kilometers away.

   a. How long did it take Brenda to reach the ferry terminal?
   b. At what speed should she drive to reach the ferry terminal 30 minutes earlier? Give your answer correct to the nearest whole number.

44. The figure shows some identical cubes stacked in a corner. The total volume of the cubes is 324 cubic centimeters. Find the length of one edge of a cube.

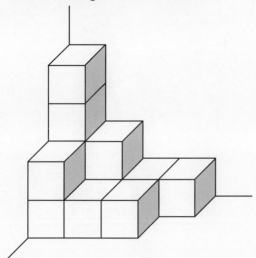

45. Stephen is making a pattern with some matchsticks.

   a. How many matchsticks does he need to form a row of 5 rectangles?

   b. How many matchsticks does he need to form a row of 21 rectangles?

Figure	1st	2nd	3rd	4th
Pattern				

End-of-Year Test G

Section A

Questions 1 to 15 carry 1 point each. For each question, choose the correct answer and write its letter in the parentheses provided.

1. If $z = 7$, what is the value of $\dfrac{z}{2} \times 18 + 3$?
   a. 12 b. 21
   c. 63 d. 66 ( )

2. What number does x represent?

   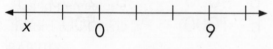

   a. −9 b. −6
   c. −2 d. 4 ( )

3. How many eighths are there in 4 wholes?
   a. 2 b. 4
   c. 8 d. 32 ( )

4. Neve bought some beads. The ratio of the number of yellow beads to green beads to purple beads is in the ratio 7 : 2 : 11. What fraction of the total number of beads are green?
   a. $\dfrac{3}{10}$ b. $\dfrac{11}{20}$
   c. $\dfrac{7}{20}$ d. $\dfrac{1}{10}$ ( )

5. Lee took a brisk walk for 2 hours at a speed of 5 kilometers per hour. How far did he walk?
   a. 2.5 km b. 3 km
   c. 7 km d. 10 km ( )

6. Name the solid formed by this net.

   a. cube
   b. cuboid
   c. trapezoidal prism
   d. triangular prism ( )

7. Dennis drove at an average speed of 50 kilometers per hour over a distance of 90 kilometers. How long did he take to reach his destination?
   a. 2.0 h b. 1.8 h
   c. 1.5 h d. 0.5 h ( )

8. Point O is at the center of this circle. Which line segment is the diameter of the circle?

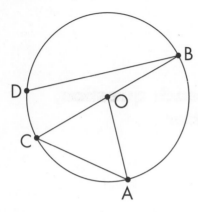

   a. $\overline{BD}$ b. $\overline{BC}$
   c. $\overline{OB}$ d. $\overline{AC}$ ( )

9. Find the area of the semicircle. (Take $\pi = 3.14$)

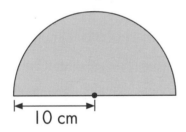

   a. 357 cm²   b. 314 cm²
   c. 157 cm²   d. 154 cm² ( )

10. Find the perimeter of the quadrant. $\left(\text{Take } \pi = \dfrac{22}{7}\right)$

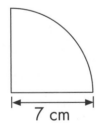

   a. 11 cm   b. 14 cm
   c. 25 cm   d. 52.5 cm ( )

This pie chart shows the bread sold by a bakery in a month. Use the chart to answer questions 11 and 12.

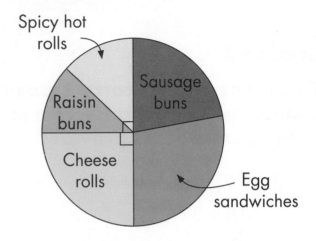

11. If 4000 pieces of bread were sold altogether, how many cheese rolls were sold?
   a. 4000   b. 2000
   c. 1000   d. 500   ( )

12. Which two types of bread combined were sold with the same quantity as cheese rolls?
   a. Spicy hot rolls and sausage buns
   b. Egg sandwiches and raisin buns
   c. Spicy hot rolls and egg sandwiches
   d. Spicy hot rolls and raisin buns
                       ( )

13. The population of Town X was 23 150 in 2009. In 2010, the population was 25 928. What was the percentage increase in the population?
a. 12%   b. 25%
c. 27%   d. 31%   (   )

14. The figure shows two squares. Find the area of the shaded part.

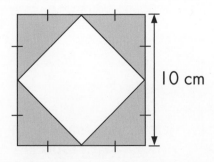

10 cm

a. 10 cm²   b. 25 cm²
c. 50 cm²   d. 100 cm² (   )

15. The figure shows an isosceles triangle and a rectangle. The area of the rectangle is 120 square centimeters. What is the perimeter of the figure?

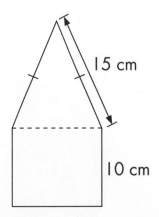

15 cm

10 cm

a. 62 cm   b. 60 cm
c. 50 cm   d. 38 cm   (   )

Section B

**For questions 16 to 35, each answer carries 1 point.
Write your answer in the answer blank provided.**

The pie chart shows the favorite fruits of a group of students.
Use the information shown to answer questions 16, 17, and 18.

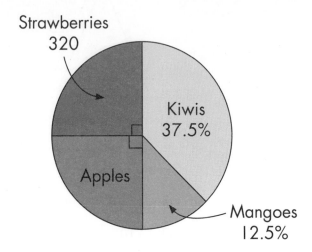

16. How many students like kiwis or mangoes?

Ans: _____ students

17. How many more students prefer strawberries over mangoes?

Ans: _____ students

18. What fraction of the students like mangoes?

Ans: _____

19. The number of cashewnuts in a bowl are $\frac{3}{7}$ the number
of walnuts. How many nuts are there in all if there are
91 walnuts in the bowl?

Ans: _____ nuts

20. The number of peaches and plums at the grocer's are in the ratio 6 : 5. If there are 78 peaches, how many more peaches than plums are there?

Ans: _____ peaches

21. A van can travel 20 kilometers in 20 minutes. Find its speed.

Ans: _____ km/h

22. The volume of a cuboid is 324 cubic centimeters. The area of its base is 36 square centimeters. Find the height of the cuboid.

Ans: _____ cm

23. The volume of a rectangular box 25 centimeters high is 30 000 cubic centimeters. What is the area of the base of the box?

Ans: _____ cm^2

24. The capacity of a rectangular tub is 8.25 liters. If the area of its base is 750 square centimeters, find the height of the tub.

Ans: _____ cm

25. If 85% of a number is 2210, what is 15% of that number?

Ans: _____

26. Bob, Irene, and Cherie shared 299 postcards. Bob received $\frac{1}{4}$ as many postcards as Irene, while Irene received $\frac{1}{2}$ as many postcards as Cherie. How many postcards did Bob receive?

Ans: _____ postcards

27. Ken traveled from Town Y to Town Z. He took 45 minutes to complete the first 80 kilometers of the journey and another 30 minutes to complete the remaining 70 kilometers. What was his average speed for the whole journey?

Ans: _____ km/h

28. A container measuring 80 centimeters by 30 centimeters by 40 centimeters is $\frac{1}{4}$-filled with water. How much water is in the container? Express your answer in liters.
($1\ L = 1000\ cm^3$)

Ans: _____ L

29. A tank measuring 80 centimeters by 40 centimeters by 40 centimeters is filled to the brim with water. Half of the water is then drained out of the tank. How many liters of water were left in the tank?
($1\ L = 1000\ cm^3$)

Ans: _____ L

30. The figure shows a square and a quadrant. Find the area of the unshaded part of the figure. $\left(\text{Take } \pi = \dfrac{22}{7} \right)$

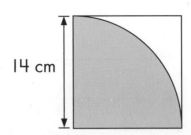

14 cm

Ans: _____ cm^2

31. The figure shows a square and a triangle. The area of the figure is 96 square centimeters. What is the area of the triangle?

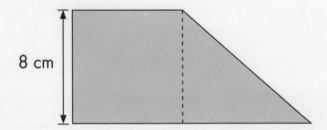

8 cm

Ans: _____ cm^2

32. The figure shows a square of side 20 centimeters and 2 semicircles. Find the perimeter of the figure. (Take $\pi = 3.14$)

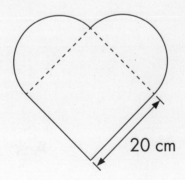

20 cm

Ans: _____ cm

33. There are 18q brooches on display. A quarter of the brooches are silver and the rest are gold. If 9 gold brooches are sold, how many gold brooches are left? Give your answer in terms of q.

Ans: _____ gold brooches

34. The figure shows a circle of diameter 28 centimeters. Find the area of the shaded part of the figure.

$\left(\text{Take } \pi = \dfrac{22}{7} \right)$

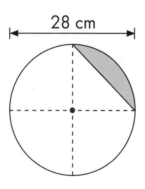

28 cm

Ans: _____ cm²

35. The figure shows the net of a cuboid. If the shaded part is the base of the cuboid, which face is the top of the cuboid?

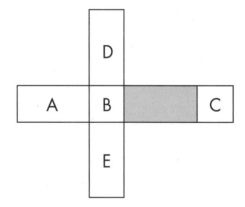

Ans: _____

Section C

For questions 36 to 45, each answer carries 1 point.
Write your answer in the space provided.
Show your work.

36. The breadth of the rectangular field is $\frac{3}{5}$ its length.

    The perimeter of the field is 320 meters.

    a. What is the length of the field?
    b. What is the area of the field?

37. The figure shows two semicircles. Find the area of the shaded part.

    $\left(\text{Take } \pi = \frac{22}{7}\right)$

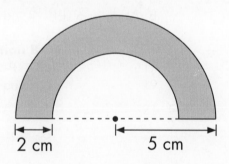

2 cm   5 cm

38. A rectangular cuboid has a base area of 108 square centimeters.
The volume of a cube is $\frac{1}{3}$ the volume of the cuboid.
Find the length of one edge of the cube.

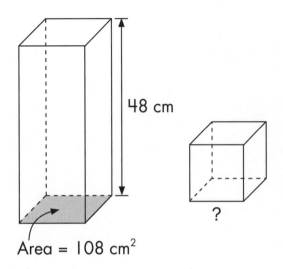

48 cm

Area = 108 cm²

?

39. A rectangular tank with a square base has a height
of 27 centimeters. Kumar filled it to the brim with
43.2 liters of water. Find the length of the base of
the tank. (1 L = 1000 cm³)

40. A rectangular container has a base area of 320 square centimeters and a height of 60 centimeters. It is $\frac{2}{3}$-filled with water. 2.9 liters of water are then poured out of the container. How many liters of water are left in the container? (1 L = 1000 cm³)

41. A van and a car left Town X for Town Y at the same time. The car traveled at an average speed of 100 kilometers per hour for the first 12 minutes and at 80 kilometers per hour for the last 2 hours. The van traveled at an average speed of 90 kilometers per hour for the entire trip.

    a. Find the distance between Town X and Town Y.
    b. Which vehicle reached Town Y first?

42. Johan drove for 4 hours to a warehouse 220 kilometers away.

   a. Find his average speed.
   b. At what speed should he drive to reach the warehouse
      20 minutes earlier?

43. The figure shows some cubes of edge 1 centimeter stacked
    in a corner. How many more 1-centimeter cubes are needed
    to make a cuboid measuring 3 centimeters by 2 centimeters
    by 4 centimeters?

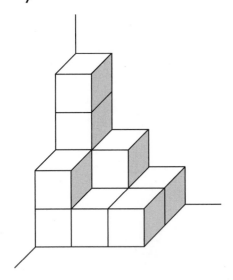

44. Theo used a piece of wire to form a figure made up of straight lines and semicircles. Each semicircle has a radius of 2 cm.

    a. Find the length of wire that he used.
    b. Find the area enclosed by the figure.
       (Take π = 3.14)

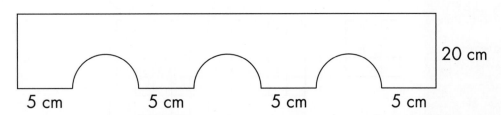

45. Anthea is forming a pattern with some tiles.

   a. How many gray tiles and white tiles are needed to form the 4th pattern?

   b. What is the total number of tiles in the 10th pattern?

Figure	1st	2nd	3rd
Pattern			

End-of-Year Test H

Section A

Questions 1 to 15 carry 1 point each. For each question, choose the correct answer and write its letter in the parentheses provided.

1. Simplify $\frac{1}{2}f + 2 - 7 + 7f$.

   a. $\frac{1}{2}f - 5$

   b. $2\frac{1}{2}f$

   c. $7\frac{1}{2}f - 5$

   d. $7\frac{1}{2}f + 9$ (   )

2. The figure below is not drawn to scale. ACDE is a parallelogram and BAE is a straight line. Find the measure of $\angle$BAC.

   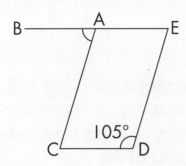

   a. 75°   b. 95°

   c. 105°   d. 120°   (   )

This pie chart shows the types of toys sold at a toy store during a sale. Use the chart to answer questions 3 and 4.

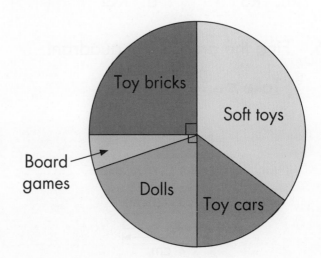

3. If 1000 soft toys and toy cars were sold, how many sets of toy bricks were sold?

   a. 500   b. 200

   c. 100   d. 50   (   )

4. Which type of toy was least popular during the sale?

   a. Soft toys

   b. Toy bricks

   c. Dolls

   d. Board games   (   )

5. Point O is at the centre of this circle. Which line segment is the radius of the circle?

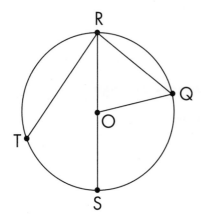

a. $\overline{RT}$ b. $\overline{OQ}$
c. $\overline{RS}$ d. $\overline{RQ}$ (   )

6. Find the area of the quadrant.
$$\left(\text{Take } \pi = \frac{22}{7} \right)$$

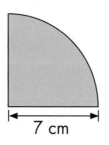

7 cm

a. 38.5 cm²
b. 77.0 cm²
c. 154.0 cm²
d. 168.5 cm²   (   )

7. Dave can stack 24 boxes in 4 minutes. At this rate, how many boxes can he stack in 1 hour?
a. 6   b. 24
c. 60   d. 360   (   )

8. Which number line shows the sum of −8 and 4?
a.
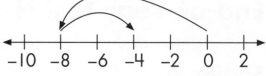

b.
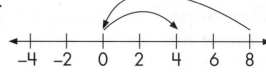

c.
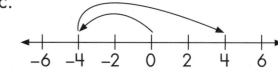

d.
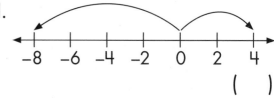

(   )

9. A sack contains 3 kilograms of fertilizer. Evan bought 2 sacks and used $\frac{3}{4}$ kilogram of fertilizer every day. How many days will he take to finish using the fertillizer?
a. 2   b. 6
c. 8   d. 12   (   )

10. The capacity of a jug is 8 times that of a cup. If their total capacity is 2.25 liters, what is the capacity of the jug?
a. 0.8 L   b. 1.5 L
c. 1.8 L   d. 2 L   (   )

11. Maria cycled from her house to the park at a speed of 6 kilometers per hour. She took 20 minutes to reach the park. How far was the park from her house?
   a. 120 km   b. 26 km
   c. 14 km   d. 2 km   ( )

12. Juwita drove from the city to her hometown 300 kilometers away. She traveled at an average speed of 100 kilometers per hour. What time will she reach her hometown if she left the city at 7.00 a.m.?
   a. 9.00 a.m.
   b. 10.00 a.m.
   c. 9.00 p.m.
   d. 10.00 p.m.   ( )

13. The figure shows a semicircle and 2 quadrants. Find the perimeter of the figure. $\left(\text{Take } \pi = \dfrac{22}{7} \right)$

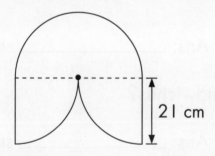

   a. 216 cm   b. 174 cm
   c. 153 cm   d. 132 cm   ( )

14. The figure shows a square and an equilateral triangle. The area of the square is 36 square centimeters. Find the perimeter of the figure.

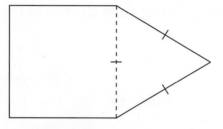

   a. 36 cm   b. 35 cm
   c. 30 cm   d. 18 cm   ( )

15. The figure shows a semicircle and a square. What is the area of the unshaded part? (Take $\pi = 3.14$)

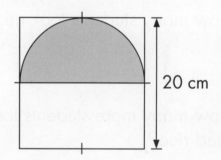

20 cm

   a. 157 cm^2
   b. 243 cm^2
   c. 314 cm^2
   d. 400 cm^2 ( )

Section B

For questions 16 to 35, each answer carries 1 point.
Write your answer in the answer blank provided.

The pie chart shows the lunch taken by 900 students.
Use the information to answer questions 16, 17, and 18.

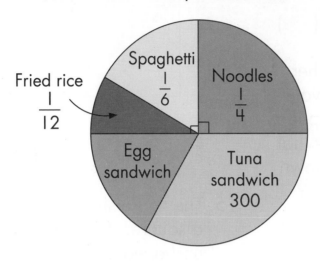

16. How many students took noodles?

Ans: _____ students

17. How many more students took tuna sandwiches than fried rice?

Ans: _____ students

18. How many students took spaghetti or egg sandwiches?

Ans: _____ students

19. A truck driver drove for 90 minutes at a speed of 75 kilometers per hour. Find the distance traveled by the truck.

Ans: _____ km

20. An electric cart can go up to 15 kilometers in 30 minutes. What is its maximum speed?

Ans: _____ km/h

21. Zul drove for 20 kilometers in 30 minutes. He then continued 40 kilometers in 40 minutes. What was his average speed?

Ans: _____ km/h

22. Meera is t years old. Her uncle is 3 times as old as her. What is their total age in 2 years' time?

Ans: _____ years

23. The number of almond tarts for sale are $\frac{2}{9}$ the number of pecan tarts. How many pecan tarts are there if there are 121 tarts in all?

Ans: _____ pecan tarts

24. The number of keychains and magnets at a souvenir store are in the ratio 11 : 7. If there are 126 magnets, how many more keychains than magnets are there?

Ans: _____ keychains

25. Zaila, Vijay, and Wayne shared 192 stickers. Zaila got $\frac{1}{5}$ as many stickers as Vijay while Vijay received $\frac{1}{2}$ as many stickers as Wayne. How many stickers did Zaila get?

Ans: _____ stickers

26. If 95% of a number is 1805, what is 22% of that number?

Ans: _____

27. The capacity of a cubical box is 729 cubic centimeters. Find the length of each edge of the box.

Ans: _____ cm

28. The volume of a cuboid is 1536 cubic centimeters and its height is 24 centimeters. What is the area of the base of the cuboid?

Ans: _____ cm²

29. A rectangular water tank can hold 15 liters of water. The base of the tank measures 40 centimeters by 25 centimeters. What is the height of the tank?
(1 L = 1000 cm³)

Ans: _____ cm

30. A tank measuring 70 centimeters by 30 centimeters by 40 centimeters is half-filled with water. How many liters of water are needed to fill the tank to the brim?
(1 L = 1000 cm³)

Ans: _____ L

31. The figure shows a three-quarter circle. Find its area.
$\left(\text{Take } \pi = \dfrac{22}{7} \right)$

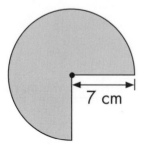

7 cm

Ans: _____ cm²

100

32. The figure shows a square and a circle. Find the area
of the unshaded part of the figure. $\left(\text{Take } \pi = \dfrac{22}{7}\right)$

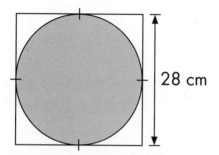

28 cm

Ans: _____ cm^2

33. The figure shows a rectangle and 2 identical quadrants.
Find the area of the unshaded part of the figure.
$\left(\text{Take } \pi = \dfrac{22}{7}\right)$

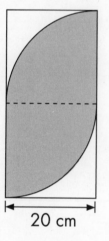

20 cm

Ans: _____ cm^2

34. The figure shows the net of a cuboid. If the shaded part is the base of the cuboid, which face is the top of the cuboid?

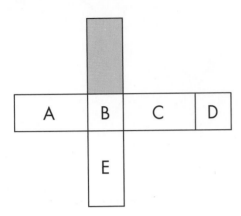

Ans: _____

35. The figure shows 2 isosceles triangles in a rectangle. The area of the rectangle is 400 square centimeters. What is the total area of the shaded parts?

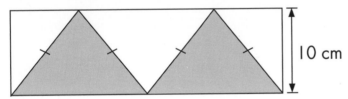

10 cm

Ans: _____ cm^2

Section C

For questions 36 to 44, each answer carries 1 point.
Write your answer in the space provided.
Show your work.

36. The number of boys at a stadium is $\frac{2}{5}$ of the number of girls. The number of girls is $\frac{1}{3}$ of the number of adults.

   a. What is the ratio of the number of boys to the number of adults at the stadium?
   b. If there are 150 adults, how many children are at the stadium?

37. A stationery kit contains 5 pens and h markers. Danny repacks the content of 14 kits equally into 7 boxes.

   a. How many pens and markers does he have in all?
   b. How many pens and markers will he pack into each of the 7 boxes?
   c. If $h = 15$, find the total number of pens and markers he has.

38. A rectangular tank has a square base of side 10 centimeters and a height of 80 centimeters. It is completely filled with water. $\frac{1}{4}$ of the water is then poured out of the tank.
How many liters of water are left in the container?
(1 L $= 1000$ cm^3)

39. The figure shows 2 identical quadrants. Find the perimeter of the figure. $\left(\text{Take } \pi = \frac{22}{7}\right)$

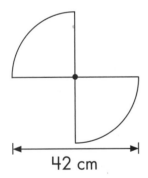

42 cm

40. The capacity of a rectangular container of height 16 centimeters is 4 times that of a cubical box of edge 8 centimeters. What is the base area of the container?

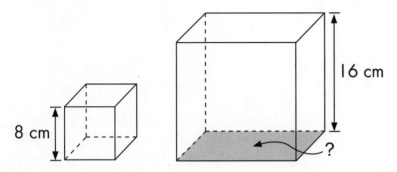

41. Jim and Sarah left Town Q for Town P at the same time.
Jim drove at an average speed of 100 kilometers per hour for 3 hours to reach Town P.
Sarah drove at an average speed of 120 kilometers per hour for the first 15 minutes and 90 kilometers per hour for the remaining distance.

a. Find the distance from Town Q to Town P.
b. Who reached Town P first?

42. The figure shows some cubes of edge 1 centimeter stacked in a corner. How many 1-centimeter cubes must be added to form a cube with each edge measuring 5 centimeters?

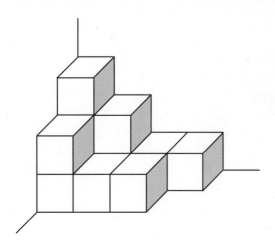

43. Suhaila used a length of wire to form the figure below.
    Each semicircle has a diameter of 6 centimeters.

    a. What is the total length of wire that she used?

    b. What is the area enclosed by the wire?
    (Take π = 3.14)

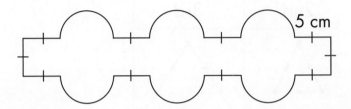

5 cm

44. Pauline is drawing a pattern on a whiteboard.

    a. How many dots will she draw for the 4th figure?
    b. How many dots will she draw for the figure
       that has 6 dots on each side?

Figure	1st	2nd	3rd
Pattern			

Skills and Strategies Index

Skills		Knowledge	Comprehension	Application
NUMBERS				
1	Four operations of whole numbers and fractions			
2	Position		Q33	
3	Negative numbers	Q16	Q12	
4	Word problems		Q26, Q32, Q37, Q40, Q41	Q43
ALGEBRA				
5	Algebraic expression in one variable	Q1, Q2, Q19		
6	Word problems		Q9, Q22, Q23, Q36	Q46
GEOMETRY				
7	Geometrical figures	Q5, Q6, Q18		
8	Nets	Q7, Q8, Q17	Q14, Q34, Q35	
RATIO				
9	Ratio and direct proportion		Q10, Q20, Q21	
10	Word problems		Q25, Q27, Q30, Q31, Q42	Q44
PERCENTAGE				
11	Using percentage			
12	Word problems		Q11, Q28, Q29, Q39	Q15, Q45
PROBABILITY				
13	Using probability	Q3, Q4		
14	Combinations		Q13	
15	Word problems		Q24, Q38	
Strategies		**Knowledge**	**Comprehension**	**Application**
1	Draw a model		Q41	
2	Simplify the problem			Q43, Q44, Q45
3	Before-after concept			Q45

Mid-Year Test B

Skills		Knowledge	Comprehension	Application
NUMBERS				
1	Four operations of whole numbers and fractions			
2	Position		Q33	
3	Negative numbers	Q3, Q16	Q13	
4	Word problems		Q10, Q25	
ALGEBRA				
5	Algebraic expression in one variable	Q1, Q2, Q19		
6	Word problems		Q26, Q27, Q36, Q39	
GEOMETRY				
7	Geometrical figures	Q5, Q9, Q18	Q42	
8	Nets	Q6, Q7, Q8, Q17	Q34, Q35	
RATIO				
9	Ratio and direct proportion		Q11, Q21, Q22, Q23	
10	Word problems		Q24, Q29, Q31, Q37, Q41	Q43, Q44
PERCENTAGE				
11	Using percentage		Q30	
12	Word problems		Q12, Q28, Q32, Q40	Q45
PROBABILITY				
13	Using probability	Q4		
14	Combinations		Q14	
15	Word problems		Q20, Q38	Q15
Strategies		**Knowledge**	**Comprehension**	**Application**
1	Draw a model			Q43, Q44, Q45
2	Before-after concept			Q45

Mid-Year Test C

Skills		Knowledge	Comprehension	Application
NUMBERS				
1	Four operations of whole numbers and fractions			
2	Position		Q14	
3	Negative numbers	Q3, Q17	Q12	
4	Word problems	Q9	Q11, Q27, Q37, Q41	Q42
ALGEBRA				
5	Algebraic expression in one variable	Q1, Q2, Q19		
6	Word problems		Q23, Q24	Q45
GEOMETRY				
7	Geometrical figures	Q6, Q18	Q34, Q36	
8	Nets	Q7, Q8, Q16	Q35	
RATIO				
9	Ratio and direct proportion		Q10, Q20, Q21	
10	Word problems		Q22, Q25, Q26, Q30, Q40	Q43
PERCENTAGE				
11	Using percentage		Q29	
12	Word problems		Q28, Q31, Q38	Q15, Q44
PROBABILITY				
13	Using probability	Q4, Q5		
14	Combinations		Q13	
15	Word problems		Q32, Q33, Q39	
Strategies		**Knowledge**	**Comprehension**	**Application**
1	Draw a model		Q40, Q41	Q43
2	Simplify the problem			Q42

Mid-Year Test D

Skills		Knowledge	Comprehension	Application
NUMBERS				
1	Four operations of whole numbers and fractions	Q4		
2	Position		Q33	
3	Negative numbers	Q3, Q16	Q14	
4	Word problems		Q10, Q25, Q31, Q38	Q42
ALGEBRA				
5	Algebraic expression in one variable	Q1, Q2, Q17		
6	Word problems		Q22, Q23, Q36, Q37	
GEOMETRY				
7	Geometrical figures	Q5	Q13, Q27	
8	Nets	Q6, Q18	Q34, Q35	
RATIO				
9	Ratio and direct proportion		Q7, Q19, Q20, Q21	
10	Word problems		Q26, Q32, Q40	Q41, Q45
PERCENTAGE				
11	Using percentage		Q30	
12	Word problems		Q11, Q12, Q28, Q29	Q43, Q44
PROBABILITY				
13	Using probability			
14	Combinations		Q15	
15	Word problems		Q8, Q9, Q24, Q39	
Strategies		**Knowledge**	**Comprehension**	**Application**
1	Draw a model			Q41, Q44, Q45
2	Simplify the problem			Q42

End of-Year Test E

Skills		Knowledge	Comprehension	Application
NUMBERS				
1	Four operations of whole numbers and fractions	Q5		
2	Position			
3	Negative numbers	Q2		
4	Word problems		Q10	
ALGEBRA				
5	Algebraic expression in one variable	Q1		
6	Word problems		Q21	
GEOMETRY				
7	Geometrical figures			
8	Nets		Q33	
RATIO				
9	Ratio and direct proportion			
10	Word problems		Q9, Q20, Q29, Q36	
PERCENTAGE				
11	Using percentage			
12	Word problems		Q19, Q22	
PROBABILITY				
13	Using probability			
14	Combinations			
15	Word problems		Q8	Q15
SPEED				
16	Distance, time, and speed			
17	Word problems		Q11, Q12, Q23, Q24, Q25, Q37, Q43	
MEASUREMENT				
18	Area and circumference of a circle	Q6, Q7	Q31, Q32	
19	Area and perimeter of composite figures		Q30, Q38	Q13, Q14, Q34, Q35, Q45
20	Volume of cube and cuboid		Q26, Q27, Q28	
21	Word problems		Q39, Q40, Q41, Q42	
DATA ANALYSIS				
22	Pie charts	Q3, Q4, Q16, Q18	Q17	
Strategies		**Knowledge**	**Comprehension**	**Application**
1	Simplify the problem		Q36	
2	Look for patterns			Q44

End of-Year Test F

	Skills	Knowledge	Comprehension	Application
NUMBERS				
1	Four operations of whole numbers and fractions			
2	Position			
3	Negative numbers	Q2		
4	Word problems		Q36	
ALGEBRA				
5	Algebraic expression in one variable	Q1		
6	Word problems		Q22	
GEOMETRY				
7	Geometrical figures			
8	Nets		Q8, Q34	
RATIO				
9	Ratio and direct proportion			
10	Word problems		Q9, Q11, Q16, Q17, Q18, Q24, Q37	
PERCENTAGE				
11	Using percentage		Q23	
12	Word problems		Q10	
PROBABILITY				
13	Using probability			
14	Combinations			
15	Word problems			
SPEED				
16	Distance, time, and speed			
17	Word problems		Q12, Q13, Q26, Q27, Q38, Q43	
MEASUREMENT				
18	Area and circumference of a circle	Q5, Q6, Q7	Q41	
19	Area and perimeter of composite figures		Q14, Q31, Q32, Q33, Q39	Q15, Q35
20	Volume of cube and cuboid		Q25, Q28, Q29, Q30, Q44	
21	Word problems		Q40, Q42	
DATA ANALYSIS				
22	Pie charts	Q4	Q3, Q19, Q20, Q21	
	Strategy	**Knowledge**	**Comprehension**	**Application**
1	Look for patterns			Q45

114

End of-Year Test G

Skills		Knowledge	Comprehension	Application
NUMBERS				
1	Four operations of whole numbers and fractions	Q3		
2	Position			
3	Negative numbers	Q2		
4	Word problems			
ALGEBRA				
5	Algebraic expression in one variable	Q1		
6	Word problems		Q33	
GEOMETRY				
7	Geometrical figures			
8	Nets	Q6	Q35	
RATIO				
9	Ratio and direct proportion			
10	Word problems		Q4, Q19, Q20, Q26, Q36	
PERCENTAGE				
11	Using percentage		Q25	
12	Word problems		Q13	
PROBABILITY				
13	Using probability			
14	Combinations			
15	Word problems			
SPEED				
16	Distance, time, and speed			
17	Word problems		Q5, Q7, Q21, Q27, Q41, Q42	
MEASUREMENT				
18	Area and circumference of a circle	Q8, Q9, Q10		Q34
19	Area and perimeter of composite figures		Q30, Q31, Q32, Q37, Q44	Q14, Q15
20	Volume of cube and cuboid		Q22, Q23, Q24, Q28, Q43	
21	Word problems		Q29, Q38, Q39, Q40	
DATA ANALYSIS				
22	Pie charts	Q18	Q11, Q12, Q16, Q17	

Strategies		Knowledge	Comprehension	Application
1	Simplify the problem		Q43	
2	Look for patterns			Q45

End of-Year Test H

	Skills	Knowledge	Comprehension	Application
NUMBERS				
1	Four operations of whole numbers and fractions			
2	Position			
3	Negative numbers		Q8	
4	Word problems		Q9	
ALGEBRA				
5	Algebraic expression in one variable	Q1		
6	Word problems		Q22, Q37	
GEOMETRY				
7	Geometrical figures	Q2		
8	Nets		Q34	
RATIO				
9	Ratio and direct proportion			
10	Word problems		Q7, Q10, Q23, Q24, Q25, Q36	
PERCENTAGE				
11	Using percentage		Q26	
12	Word problems			
PROBABILITY				
13	Using probability			
14	Combinations			
15	Word problems			
SPEED				
16	Distance, time, and speed			
17	Word problems		Q11, Q12, Q19, Q20, Q21, Q41	
MEASUREMENT				
18	Area and circumference of a circle	Q5, Q6	Q13, Q31, Q39	
19	Area and perimeter of composite figures		Q32, Q33, Q43	Q14, Q15, Q35
20	Volume of cube and cuboid		Q27, Q28, Q29, Q30, Q42	
21	Word problems		Q38, Q40	
DATA ANALYSIS				
22	Pie charts	Q4	Q3, Q16, Q17, Q18	

	Strategies	Knowledge	Comprehension	Application
1	Simplify the problem		Q42	
2	Look for patterns			Q44

Answer Key

Mid-Year Test A

Section A
1. c	2. a	3. b	4. d
5. b	6. d	7. c	8. b
9. a	10. d	11. c	12. b
13. a	14. b	15. d	

Section B
16. –2	17. cuboid
18. 55	19. 79
20. $\frac{1}{6}$	21. $2\frac{1}{2}$
22. $6x + 20$	23. $75 - 14n$
24. $\frac{1}{50}$	25. 40
26. 6	27. $5 : 1 : 3$
28. 25	29. 20
30. $3 : 2$	31. 144
32. 16	33. Brad
34. triangles, rectangles	
35. 3	

Section C

36. Shane $\longrightarrow q$
Kate $\longrightarrow 3q$
Amanda $\longrightarrow 3q - 4$
Ray $\longrightarrow 3q - 4 - 4$
$= 3q - 8$
Ray is **($3q - 8$) years old**.

37. a. $15 \div \frac{2}{3} = 22\frac{1}{2} \approx 22$
She can get **22 pieces**.

b. $22 \times \frac{2}{3} = 14\frac{2}{3}$
$15 - 14\frac{2}{3} = \frac{1}{3}$
There is $\frac{1}{3}$ **meter** of ribbon left over.

38. a. Total number of marbles
$\longrightarrow 3 + 5 + 6 + 2 = 16$
Number of red or yellow marble
$\longrightarrow 3 + 6 = 9$
Probability of drawing red or yellow marble
$\longrightarrow \frac{9}{16}$
The probability of drawing a red marble or a yellow marble is $\frac{9}{16}$.

b. Total number of marbles
$\longrightarrow 16 + 2 = 18$
Number of red or green marble
$\longrightarrow 3 + 5 + 2 = 10$
Probability of drawing red or green marble
$\longrightarrow \frac{10}{18} = \frac{5}{9}$
The probability of drawing a red marble or a green marble is $\frac{5}{9}$.

39. Members in 2011 $\longrightarrow 115\% \times 300 = 345$
Members in 2012 $\longrightarrow 80\% \times 345 = 276$
There were **276 members** in 2012.

40. $1 - \frac{1}{8} - \frac{1}{5} = \frac{27}{40}$
$\frac{1}{3} \times \frac{27}{40} = \frac{9}{40}$
Fraction spent on notepads
$\longrightarrow 1 - \frac{1}{8} - \frac{1}{5} - \frac{9}{40}$
$= \frac{9}{20}$
Cost of each notepad $\longrightarrow \frac{9}{20} \div 3$
$= \frac{9}{20} \times \frac{1}{3}$
$= \frac{3}{20}$
Each notepad was $\frac{3}{20}$ of the money.

41. Strategy: Draw a model

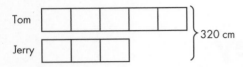

8 units → 320
3 units → 320 ÷ 8 × 3
 = 120
Jerry's height is **120 centimeters**.

42. a. Ratio of stuffed animals to dolls → 3 : 5
 Ratio of stuffed animals to dolls to total
 → 3 : 5 : (3 + 5)
 = 3 : 5 : 8
 The ratio is **3 : 5 : 8**.

 b. 3 units → 36
 1 unit → 36 ÷ 3 = 12
 8 units → 8 × 12 = 96
 There are **96 toys** altogether.

43. Strategy: Simplify the problem
 Mass of 4 lemon pies and 4 cherry pies
 → 900 × 4 = 3600
 Mass of 2 lemon pies → 4800 − 3600
 = 1200

 1200 g = 1 kg 200 g
 The mass of 2 lemon pies is
 1 kilogram 200 grams.

44. Method 1:

Parrots	:	Canaries	:	Finches
3	:	4		
		6	:	1
9	:	12	:	2

Method 2:
Strategy: Draw a model

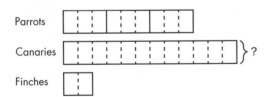

11 units → 66
1 unit → 66 ÷ 11 = 6
12 units → 6 × 12 = 72
There are **72 canaries**.

45. Strategies: Before-after concept, draw a model

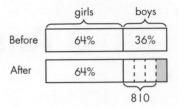

$\frac{3}{4}$ of 36% → 810

$\frac{4}{4}$ of 36% → 810 ÷ 3 × 4 = 1080

100% → 1080 ÷ 36 × 100 = 3000
There were **3000 students** in the hall at first.

46. a. Length of Rectangle T
 → 3 × r = 3r
 Perimeter of Rectangle T
 → r + r + 3r + 3r = 8r
 Perimeter of Square S
 → 3 × 8r = 24r
 The perimeter of Square S is **24r centimeters**.

 b. Perimeter of Square S → 24r
 = 24 × 5
 = 120 cm
 Edge of Square S → 120 ÷ 4 = 30 cm
 Area of Square S → 30 × 30 = 900 cm²
 The area of Square S is
 900 square centimeters.

Mid-Year Test B

Section A
1. c   2. d   3. c   4. b
5. a   6. c   7. d   8. b
9. b   10. a   11. a   12. b
13. c   14. d   15. c

Section B
16. −10   17. prism
18. 70   19. 16
20. black   21. $\frac{9}{4}$
22. $1\frac{3}{4}$ 23. 8 : 9 : 17
24. 10   25. 16
26. 18q − 5   27. 50j + 73
28. 40   29. 77
30. 490   31. 285
32. 60   33. Beth
34. 4
35. trapezoids, rectangles

118

Section C

36. a. Perimeter = $a + a + 9 = 2a + 9$
    The perimeter is **(2a + 9) centimeters**.

    b. Area = $\frac{1}{2} \times 6 \times 6 = 18$
    The area is **18 square centimeters**.

37. $2 + 3 + 2 = 7$
    7 units → 133
    3 units → $133 \div 7 \times 3 = 57$
    The longest side is **57 centimeters** long.

38. a. $8 + 11 + 7 + 4 = 30$
    $11 + 4 = 15$
    $\frac{15}{30} = \frac{1}{2}$
    The probability is $\frac{1}{2}$.

    b. $30 + 4 = 34$
    $8 + 4 + 4 = 16$
    $\frac{16}{34} = \frac{8}{17}$
    The probability is $\frac{8}{17}$.

39. a. $12 \times v = 12v$
    $12 \times 5 = 60$
    He has **12v crayons and 60 markers**.

    b. $12v \div 6 = 2v$
    $60 \div 6 = 10$
    There will be **2v crayons and 10 markers** in each box.

40. In March → 120
    In May → $120 \times 85\% = 102$
    In December → $102 \times 150\% = 153$
    There were **153 students** in the club by December.

41. a. 10 units → 550
    7 units → $550 \div 10 \times 7 = 385$
    There are **385 travel guides**.

    b. $550 - 385 = 165$
    $165 + 110 = 275$
    $275 : 385 = 5 : 7$
    The ratio is **5 : 7**.

42. a. $180° - 40° - 40° = 100°$
    The measure of $\angle$XWZ is **100°**.

    b. $\angle$ZXY = 40°
    $\angle$XZV = 40° − 10° = 30°
    $\angle$XVZ = 180° − 40° − 30° = 110°
    The measure of $\angle$XVZ is **110°**.

43. Strategy: Draw a model

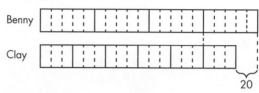

    2 units → 20
    38 units → $20 \div 2 \times 38 = 380$
    They have **380 stamps** in all.

44. Method 1:

Cherry	:	Pecan	:	Key lime
7	:	9		
		3	:	1
7	:	9	:	3

    Method 2:
    Strategy: Draw a model

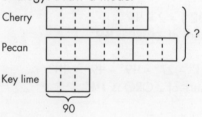

    $7 + 9 = 16$
    3 units → 90
    16 units → $90 \div 3 \times 30 = 480$
    480 cherry pies and pecan pies were sold in all.

45. Strategies: Before-after concept, draw a model

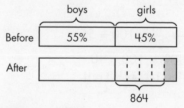

    80% → 864
    100% → $864 \div 8 \times 100 = 1080$
    There were 1080 girls.
    45% → 1080
    100% → $1080 \div 45 \times 100 = 2400$
    There were **2400 boys and girls**.

119

Mid-Year Test C

Section A

1. c	2. a	3. d	4. a
5. c	6. b	7. a	8. d
9. c	10. a	11. a	12. d
13. d	14. d	15. b	

Section B

16. cube

17. –6

18. 150

19. 36

20. $1\frac{2}{5}$

21. $\frac{3}{8}$

22. $\frac{2}{3}$

23. $12c + 2400$

24. $32p - 11$

25. 33

26. 132

27. 6

28. 10

29. 165

30. 3 : 1 : 1

31. 9 : 20

32. $\frac{1}{3}$

33. $\frac{7}{13}$

34. 60

35. 4

Section C

36. a. $(180° - 82°) \div 2 = 49°$

The measure of $\angle$ORP is **49°**.

b. $180° - 41° - 27° - 49° - 49° = 14°$

The measure of $\angle$QRO is **14°**.

37. a. $128 \div \frac{5}{12} = 307\frac{1}{5} \approx 307$

He can cut **307 pieces**.

b. $\frac{1}{5} \times \frac{5}{12} = \frac{1}{12}$

There will be $\frac{1}{12}$ **meter** of fabric left over.

38. Louise's beads $\longrightarrow \frac{11}{20} \times 100 = 55$

Remainder $\longrightarrow 40\% \times 100 = 40$

Gave to Louise $\longrightarrow 10\% \times 40 = 4$

$55 + 4 = 59$

Louise had **59 beads**.

39. a. Total number of buttons

$\longrightarrow 8 + 3 + 5 + 2 = 18$

Total number of non-purple buttons

$\longrightarrow 8 + 3 + 2 = 13$

The probability is $\frac{13}{18}$.

b. Total number of buttons $\longrightarrow 18 - 8 = 10$

Total number of non-blue buttons $\longrightarrow 5 + 2 = 7$

The probability is $\frac{7}{10}$.

40. Method 1:

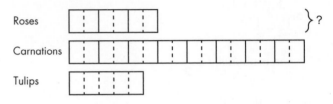

Roses	:	Carnations	:	Tulips
3	:	8		
6			:	5
6	:	16	:	5

Method 2:

Strategy: Draw a model

$16 + 5 = 21$

21 units $\longrightarrow 462$

6 units $\longrightarrow 462 \div 21 \times 6 = 132$

There are **132 roses**.

41. Strategy: Draw a model

a. 5 units $\longrightarrow 60$

2 units $\longrightarrow 60 \div 5 \times 2 = 24$

She read **24 pages** on Sunday.

b. 12 units $\longrightarrow 24 \div 2 \times 12 = 144$

There were **144 pages** in the book.

42. Strategy: Simplify the problem

5 bookends + 5 notepads

$\longrightarrow 600 \times 5 = 3000$ g

$4200 - 3000 = 1200$ g

$1200 \div 3 = 400$ g

Each bookend has a mass of **400 grams**.

43. Strategy: Draw a model

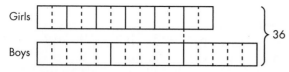

Girls

Boys

} 36

27 units ⟶ 36
12 units ⟶ 36 ÷ 27 × 12 = 16
There are **16 girls**.

44. 5 × 160% = 8
8 × 150% = 12
New ratio of white eggs to brown eggs to total
number of eggs
⟶ 8 : 12 : 20 = 2 : 3 : 5
Ratio of brown eggs to total number of eggs
⟶ 3 : 5 = 6 : 10
Percentage of brown eggs = 60%
60% of the eggs are brown.

45. a. Perimeter of square plot ⟶ 4 × d = 4d
   Length of rectangular plot
   ⟶ (4d − 4) ÷ 2 = (2d − 2)
   The length is **(2d − 2) meters**.

   b. Length = 2 × 8 − 2 = 14
   Area = 2 × 14 = 28
   The area is **28 square meters**.

Mid-Year Test D

Section A

1. b	2. d	3. c	4. d
5. b	6. d	7. a	8. a
9. b	10. a	11. c	12. c
13. b	14. c	15. d	

Section B

16. −4
17. 38
18. prism
19. 2
20. $\frac{2}{3}$
21. 5 : 16
22. 16w − 5
23. 108t + 10
24. $\frac{3}{8}$
25. 15
26. 34
27. 120
28. 600
29. $41\frac{2}{3}$
30. 1275
31. $\frac{2}{45}$
32. 112
33. Miles
34. 4
35. triangle, rectangle

Section C

36. a. 3 units ⟶ 9u
   2 units ⟶ 9u ÷ 3 × 2 = 6u
   There were **6u women**.

   b. 9u + 6u = 15u
   There were **15u people** in all.

37. a. 4x + 4x + x + x = 10x
   The perimeter is **10x centimeters**.

   b. Length = 4 × 28 = 112
   Area = 112 × 28 = 3136
   Its area is **3136 square centimeters**.

38. $4\frac{2}{3} - 1\frac{3}{4} - 2\frac{1}{2} = \frac{5}{12}$
   $\frac{5}{12} \div 3 = \frac{5}{36}$
   She used $\frac{5}{36}$ **meter** of ribbon for each brooch.

39. a. Total number of bells ⟶ 4 + 7 + 3 + 5 = 19
   Total number of non-pink bells
   ⟶ 19 − 7 = 12
   The probability is $\frac{12}{19}$.

   b. Total number of bells ⟶ 19 + 5 = 24
   Total number of non-pink bells
   ⟶ 12 + 5 = 17
   The probability is $\frac{17}{24}$.

40. a. 9 − 5 = 4
   9 units ⟶ 1944
   4 units ⟶ 1944 ÷ 9 × 4 = 864
   864 more backpacks than pouches were
   made.

   b. 5 units ⟶ 1944 ÷ 9 × 5 = 1080
   1080 × 12 = 12 960
   12 960 pouches are made in a year.

41. a. Method 1:

China	:	India	:	Kenya
5	:	4		
		6	:	5
15	:	12	:	10

Method 2:
Strategy: Draw a model

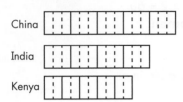

The store imported the greatest number of boxes from **China**.

b. 15 + 12 + 10 = 37
    15 units ⟶ 1290
    1 unit ⟶ 1290 ÷ 15
             = 86
    37 units ⟶ 86 × 37 = 3182
    The store imported **3182 boxes** of tea in all.

42. Strategy: Simplify the problem
    1 bus and 1 van ⟶ 72
    3 buses and 3 vans ⟶ 72 × 3 = 216
    1 bus ⟶ 276 − 216 = 60
    Each bus can carry **60 children**.

43. 6 units × 125% = 7.5 units
    5 units × 120% = 6 units
    7.5 : 6 = 15 : 12 = 5 : 4
    The ratio now is **5 : 4**.

44. Strategy: Draw a model

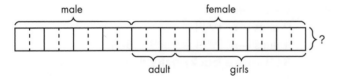

    9 units ⟶ 180
    20 units ⟶ 180 ÷ 9 × 20 = 400
    There were **400 guests** at the party.

45. Strategy: Draw a model

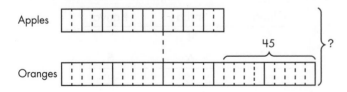

    25 − 16 = 9
    16 + 25 = 41
    9 units ⟶ 45
    41 units ⟶ 45 ÷ 9 × 41 = 205
    There are **205 apples and oranges** in all.

End-of-Year Test E

Section A
1. d	2. a	3. b	4. d
5. d	6. c	7. a	8. b
9. c	10. a	11. b	12. c
13. a	14. d	15. b	

Section B
16. 600	17. 200
18. 400	19. 35
20. 98	21. 200s + 7
22. 25	23. 182
24. 6	25. 72
26. 53.6	27. 63
28. 30	29. 25
30. 135	31. 77
32. 44	33. B
34. $21\frac{3}{7}$	35. 125

Section C
36. a. Strategy: Simplify the problem

Table	:	Cabinet	:	Stool
5	:	6		
		4	:	1
10	:	12	:	3

The ratio is **10 : 12 : 3**.

    b. 10 + 12 + 3 = 25 units
        3 units ⟶ 4.5 kg
        1 unit ⟶ 4.5 ÷ 3 = 1.5 kg
        25 units ⟶ 25 × 1.5 = 37.5 kg
        37.5 ÷ 3 = 12.5 kg
        The average mass is **12.5 kilograms**.

37. a. Total distance = (80 × 0.5) + (75 × 2)
                      = 40 + 150
                      = 190 km
       The distance is **190 kilometers**.

    b. Total time taken = 30 min + 2 h = 2 h 30 min
       2 hours 30 minutes after 10.25 a.m. is
       12.55 p.m.
       The car reached Town B at **12.55 p.m.**

122

38. Area of unshaded part
= Area of square – Area of 4 circles
Area of square = 14×14
$= 196$ cm^2
Area of circles = $4 \times \dfrac{22}{7} \times \dfrac{7}{2} \times \dfrac{7}{2}$
$= 154$ cm^2
Area of unshaded part = $196 - 154$
$= 42$ cm^2
The area is **42 square centimeters**.

39. Volume of water at first = $24 \times 10 \times 40 \times \dfrac{1}{4}$
$= 2400$ cm^3
Volume of water in the end = $2400 + 400$
$= 2800$ cm^3
2800 cm^3 = 2.8 L
There are **2.8 liters** of water in the container.

40. Volume = $20 \times 5 \times 10 = 1000$ cm^3
Length of edge of cube = $\sqrt[3]{1000} = 10$ cm
The length of one edge of the cube is
10 centimeters.

41. $0.512 \times 1000 = 512$
Length of one edge = $\sqrt[3]{512} = 8$ cm
Area of base = $8 \times 8 = 64$ cm^2
The area of the base is **64 square centimeters**.

42. a. 1.32 L = 1320 cm^3
Area of base = 22×15
$= 330$ cm^2
Height = $1320 \div 330$
$= 4$ cm
The height of the water level is **4 centimeters**.

b. Capacity of container = 10×330
$= 3300$ cm^3
Volume of water needed = $3300 - 1320$
$= 1980$ cm^3
1.98 liters of water are needed.

43. a. Time taken = $120 \div 80 = 1.5$ h
He took **1.5 hours** to reach his office.

b. 1.5 h = 90 min
$90 - 15 = 75$ min
He should take 75 minutes to travel.
Speed = $120 \div \dfrac{75}{60} = 96$ km/h
He should drive at **96 kilometers per hour**.

44. Strategy: Look for patterns

Figure	Toothpicks	Pattern
1	4	$4 + (3 \times 0)$
2	$4 + 3$	$4 + (3 \times 1)$
3	$4 + 3 + 3$	$4 + (3 \times 2)$
4	$4 + 3 + 3 + 3$	$4 + (3 \times 3)$

a. Figure 12 $\longrightarrow$ $4 + (3 \times 11) = 37$
He needs **37 toothpicks**.

b. Figure 24 $\longrightarrow$ $4 + (3 \times 23) = 73$
He needs **73 toothpicks**.

45. Shaded part in small square
= $2 \times$ (Area of quadrant — Area of triangle)
$= 2 \times \left(\dfrac{1}{4} \times 3.14 \times 2 \times 2 - \dfrac{1}{2} \times 2 \times 2 \right)$
$= 2.28$ cm^2
Unshaded part = $(4 \times 4) - 2.28 = 13.72$ cm^2
The area of the unshaded part is
13.72 square centimeters.

End-of-Year Test F

Section A
1. b   2. b   3. d   4. a
5. d   6. d   7. b   8. d
9. d   10. a   11. c   12. b
13. a   14. c   15. b

Section B
16. $2 : 7 : 9$ 17. $1 : 2$
18. 9   19. 360
20. 2880   21. 720
22. $11\dfrac{1}{3}v$ 23. 720
24. 18   25. 7
26. 67.5   27. 90
28. 1701   29. 42.5
30. 68.4   31. $519\dfrac{3}{4}$
32. 40   33. 122.8
34. C   35. 49.5

Section C
36. a. $29 \div \dfrac{4}{7} = 50\dfrac{3}{4}$
She can cut **50 strips**.

b. $50 \times \frac{4}{7} = 28\frac{4}{7}$

$29 - 28\frac{4}{7} = \frac{3}{7}$

There is $\frac{3}{7}$ **meter** of cloth left over.

37.

Apples	:	Plums	:	Lemons
3	:	8		
		2	:	3
3	:	8	:	12

a. 12 units ⟶ 84
   1 unit ⟶ 84 ÷ 12 = 7
   3 units ⟶ 7 × 3 = 21
   8 units ⟶ 7 × 8 = 56
   56 – 21 = 35
   There are **35 more plums** than apples.

b. 3 + 8 + 12 = 23 units
   23 units ⟶ 7 × 23 = 161
   There are **161 fruits** in all.

38. 1 h 10 min = $1\frac{1}{6}$ h

40 min = $\frac{2}{3}$ h

Distance = $\left(70 \times 1\frac{1}{6}\right) + \left(50 \times \frac{2}{3}\right)$

$= 81\frac{2}{3} + 33\frac{1}{3}$

$= 115$ km

Town A and Town B are **115 kilometers apart**.

39. Area of square = 28 × 28 = 784 cm²
   Area of 4 quadrants = Area of circle

$= \frac{22}{7} \times 14 \times 14$

$= 616$ cm²

   Area of unshaded part = 784 – 616 = 168 cm²
   The area of the unshaded part is
   168 square centimeters.

40. Volume of water at first = $32 \times 20 \times 40 \times \frac{1}{4}$

   = 6400 cm³
   Volume of water left = 6400 – 600
   = 5800 cm³
   There are **5.8 liters** of water left.

41. Area of circle = 3.14 × 8 × 8 = 200.96 m²
   Area of a quadrant = 200.96 ÷ 4 = 50.24 m²

   Area of triangle = $\frac{1}{2} \times 8 \times 8 = 32$ m²

   Area of shaded part = 50.24 – 32 = 18.24 m²
   The area of the shaded part is
   18.24 square meters.

42. a. Volume of water = 6 × 6 × 6 × 2 = 432 cm³
   There were **432 cubic centimeters** of water in
   the container.

   b. Height = 432 ÷ (9 × 6) = 432 ÷ 54 = 8
   The height of the container is **8 centimeters**.

43. a. Time taken = $175 \div 75 = 2\frac{1}{3}$ h

   = 2 h 20 min
   She took **2 hours 20 minutes** to reach the
   ferry terminal.

   b. 2 h 20 min = 1 h 80 min
   1 h 80 min – 30 min = 1 h 50 min

   $= 1\frac{5}{6}$ h

   She should take $1\frac{5}{6}$ h to travel.

   Speed = $175 \div 1\frac{5}{6} = 95.455 \approx 95$ km/h

   She should drive at about
   95 kilometers per hour.

44. Total number of cubes = 12
   Volume of each cube = 324 ÷ 12 = 27
   Edge of cube = $\sqrt[3]{27}$ = 3
   The length of one edge of a cube is **3 centimeters**.

45. Strategy: Look for patterns

Fig.	Rectangles	Matchsticks	Pattern
1	1	6	6 + (5 × 0)
2	2	6 + 5	6 + (5 × 1)
3	3	6 + 5 + 5	6 + (5 × 2)
4	4	6 + 5 + 5 + 5	6 + (5 × 3)

a. 5 rectangles ⟶ 6 + (5 × 4) = 26
   He needs **26 matchsticks** to form 5 rectangles.

b. 21 rectangles ⟶ 6 + (5 × 20) = 106
   He needs **106 matchsticks** to form
   21 rectangles.

End-of-Year Test G

Section A

1. d	2. b	3. d	4. d
5. d	6. d	7. b	8. b
9. c	10. c	11. c	12. d
13. a	14. c	15. a	

Section B

16. 640

17. 160

18. $\frac{1}{8}$

19. 130

20. 13

21. 60

22. 9

23. 1200

24. 11

25. 390

26. 23

27. 120

28. 24

29. 64

30. 42

31. 32

32. 102.8

33. $13\frac{1}{2}q - 9$

34. 56

35. A

Section C

36. a. Ratio of breadth to length = 3 : 5
$3 + 5 + 3 + 5 = 16$ units
16 units $\longrightarrow$ 320 m
1 unit $\longrightarrow$ 320 ÷ 16 = 20 m
5 units $\longrightarrow$ 5 × 20 = 100 m
The length of the field is **100 meters**.

b. 3 units $\longrightarrow$ 3 × 20 = 60 m
The breadth of the field is 60 m.
Area = 100 × 60 = 6000 m²
The area of the field is **6000 square meters**.

37. Area of figure
$$= \left(\frac{1}{2} \times \frac{22}{7} \times 5 \times 5\right) - \left(\frac{1}{2} \times \frac{22}{7} \times 3 \times 3\right)$$
$$= 39\frac{2}{7} - 14\frac{1}{7} = 25\frac{1}{7} \text{ cm}^2$$
The area of the figure is
$25\frac{1}{7}$ **square centimeters**.

38. Volume of cuboid = 108 × 48 = 5184 cm³
Volume of cube = $\frac{1}{3} \times 5184 = 1728$ cm³
Length of edge = $\sqrt[3]{1728} = 12$ cm
The length of one edge of the cube is
12 centimeters.

39. Area of square base = 43 200 ÷ 27 = 1600 cm²
Length of base = $\sqrt{1600}$ = 40 cm
The length of the base is **40 centimeters**.

40. Capacity of container = 320 × 60
    = 19 200 cm³
Volume of water at first = $\frac{2}{3} \times$ 19 200
    = 12 800 cm³
    = 12.8 L
Volume of water left = 12.8 – 2.9
    = 9.9 L
There are **9.9 liters** of water left.

41. a. Distance traveled by car
$$= \left(100 \times \frac{12}{60}\right) + (80 \times 2)$$
= 20 + 160
= 180 km
The distance is **180 kilometers**.

b. Time taken by car = $\frac{12}{60} + 2 = 2\frac{1}{5}$ h
Time taken by van = 180 ÷ 90 = 2 h
The **van** reached first.

42. a. Speed = 220 ÷ 4 = 55
His average speed was
55 kilometers per hour.

b. 4 h – 20 min $\longrightarrow$ 3 h 60 min – 20 min
    = 3 h 40 min = $3\frac{2}{3}$ h

He should take $3\frac{2}{3}$ hours.

Speed = 220 ÷ $3\frac{2}{3}$ = 60

He should drive at **60 kilometers per hour**.

43. Strategy: Simplify the problem
Existing number of 1-cm cubes = 6 + 3 + 1 + 1
    = 11
Number of 1-cm cubes needed to form cuboid
= 3 × 2 × 4 = 24
Number of 1-cm cubes needed = 24 – 11 = 13
13 cubes are needed.

44. a. Length of straight edges
$$= (5 \times 4) + (20 \times 2) + (5 \times 4) + (2 \times 6)$$
$$= 92 \text{ cm}$$
Length of curved edges
$$= 1.5 \times 2 \times 3.14 \times 2$$
$$= 18.84 \text{ cm}$$
Total length = 92 + 18.84 = 110.84 cm
He used **110.84 centimeters** of wire.

b. Length of figure $= (5 \times 4) + (2 \times 6)$
$$= 32 \text{ cm}$$
Area $= (20 \times 32) - (1.5 \times 3.14 \times 2 \times 2)$
$$= 640 - 18.84$$
$$= 621.16$$
The area is **621.16 square centimeters**.

45. Strategy: Look for patterns

Pattern	Gray tiles	White tiles	Total
1	$1 = 1^2$	$8 = 4 \times (1 + 1)$	$9 = 3^2$
2	$4 = 2^2$	$12 = 4 \times (2 + 1)$	$16 = 4^2$
3	$9 = 3^2$	$16 = 4 \times (3 + 1)$	$25 = 5^2$

a. Number of gray tiles $= 4^2 = 16$
Number of white tiles $= 4 \times (4 + 1) = 20$
16 gray tiles and 20 white tiles are needed.

b. Total tiles $= (10 + 2)^2 = 144$ tiles
There are **144 tiles** in the 10th pattern.

End-of-Year Test H

Section A

1. c   2. a   3. a   4. d
5. b   6. a   7. d   8. a
9. c   10. d   11. d   12. b
13. b   14. c   15. b

Section B

16. 225   17. 225
18. 300   19. $112\frac{1}{2}$
20. 30   21. $51\frac{3}{7}$
22. $4t + 4$ 23. 99
24. 72   25. 12
26. 418   27. 9
28. 64   29. 15
30. 42   31. $115\frac{1}{2}$

32. 168   33. $171\frac{3}{7}$
34. E   35. 200

Section C

36. a.

Boys	:	Girls	:	Adults
2	:	5		
		1	:	3
2	:	5	:	15

The ratio is **2 : 15**.

b. 15 units ⟶ 150
1 unit ⟶ 150 ÷ 15 = 10
2 + 5 = 7
7 units ⟶ 10 × 7 = 70
There are **70 children** at the stadium.

37. a. $5 \times 14 = 70$
$h \times 14 = 14h$
He has **70 pens and 14h markers**.

b. $70 \div 7 = 10$
$14h \div 7 = 2h$
He will pack **10 pens and 2h markers** into each of the boxes.

c. $14 \times 15 = 210$
$210 + 70 = 280$
He has **280 pens and markers** in all.

38. Volume of water $= 10 \times 10 \times 80 = 8000 \text{ cm}^3$
Volume remaining $= \frac{3}{4} \times 8000$
$$= 6000 \text{ cm}^3 = 6 \text{ L}$$
There are 6 liters of water left.

39. Perimeter $= 42 + 42 + \left(\frac{1}{2} \times \frac{22}{7} \times 42 \right)$
$$= 150 \text{ cm}$$
The perimeter of the figure is **150 centimeters**.

40. Capacity of box $= 8 \times 8 \times 8 = 512 \text{ cm}^3$
Capacity of container $= 512 \times 4 = 2048 \text{ cm}^3$
Base area $= 2048 \div 16 = 128 \text{ cm}^2$
The base area of the container is **128 square centimeters**.

41. a. Distance $= 100 \times 3 = 300$
The distance is **300 kilometers**.

b. Distance driven in 1st part of journey

$= 120 \times \dfrac{15}{60} = 30$ km

Distance driven in 2nd part of journey
$= 300 - 30 = 270$ km

Time taken by Sarah $= \dfrac{15}{60} + \dfrac{270}{90} = 3\dfrac{1}{4}$ h

Time taken by Jim $= 3$ h

Jim reached Town P first.

42. Strategy: Simplify the problem
Existing number of 1-cm cubes $= 7 + 3 + 1 = 11$
Number of 1-cm cubes needed to form cube
$= 5 \times 5 \times 5 = 125$
Number of 1-cm cubes needed
$= 125 - 11 = 114$
114 cubes are needed.

43. a. Length of straight edges $= 10 \times 5 = 50$ cm
Length of curved edges
$=$ Perimeter of 3 circles
$= 3 \times 3.14 \times 6$
$= 56.52$ cm
Total length $= 50 + 56.52 = 106.52$ cm
She used **106.52 centimeters** of wire.

b. Length of rectangle $= (5 \times 4) + (6 \times 3)$
$\qquad\qquad\qquad\quad = 38$ cm
Total area $=$ Area of of rectangle $+$
$\qquad\qquad\quad$ Area of 3 circles
$\qquad\qquad = (5 \times 38) + (3 \times 3.14 \times 3 \times 3)$
$\qquad\qquad = 190 + 84.78$
$\qquad\qquad = 274.78$ cm^2
The enclosed area is
274.78 square centimeters.

44. Strategy: Look for patterns

Figure	Dots on side	Total dots	Pattern
1	2	3	3×1
2	3	6	3×2
3	4	9	3×3

a. Pattern $\longrightarrow 3 \times 4 = 12$
She will draw **12 dots**.

b. 6 dots on side $\longrightarrow 6 - 1 = 5$
She will draw the 5th figure.
Pattern $\longrightarrow 3 \times 5 = 15$
She will draw **15 dots**.